THE OFFICIAL Harry Potter BAKING BOOK

THE OFFICIAL
Harry Potter
BAKING BOOK

BY
Joanna Farrow

SCHOLASTIC INC.

WIZARDING WORLD

CONTENTS

WELCOME 6
KITCHEN SAFETY 8

SAVORY 10

Lightning Bolt Breads ⚡⚡ 12
Wand Breadsticks ⚡⚡ 14
Mimbulus Mimbletonia Bagel Loaf ⚡⚡⚡ ... 16
Salazar Slytherin's Sourdough Snake ⚡⚡⚡ ... 18
Wizarding Hats ⚡ 22
Hogwarts Crest Pie ⚡⚡⚡⚡ 24
Nimbus 2000 Crackers ⚡⚡ 26
Great Lake Tart ⚡⚡⚡ 28
Savory Owl Muffins ⚡⚡ 30
Pumpkin Patch Pies ⚡⚡ 32
Nicolas Flamel's Parcels ⚡⚡ 34
Deathly Hallows Bread ⚡⚡ 36
Devil's Snare Pretzel ⚡⚡⚡ 38
Quidditch Pitch Focaccia ⚡⚡⚡ 40
Halloumi Howlers ⚡⚡⚡ 44
Whomping Willow Cheese Straw ⚡ ... 46
Dark Detector Scones ⚡⚡ 48
Time-Turner Crackers ⚡⚡⚡ 50
Platform Nine and Three-Quarters
Polenta Bake ⚡⚡ 52
Great Hall Chicken Pie ⚡⚡ 56
Yorkshire Delights ⚡ 58
Dragon-Roasted-Nut Tarts ⚡⚡ 60

WIZARDING SKILL LEVEL

To help guide you, we've given each of our recipes a lightning bolt difficulty rating, from one (beginner) all the way up to five (complex).

⚡ BEGINNER
⚡⚡ EASY
⚡⚡⚡ INTERMEDIATE
⚡⚡⚡⚡ ADVANCED
⚡⚡⚡⚡⚡ COMPLEX

SWEET 62

- Luna's Spectrespecs Cookies 🚩🚩🚩 64
- Gryffindor Sword Cookies 🚩🚩🚩 66
- Hogwarts Gingerbread Castle 🚩🚩🚩🚩🚩 68
- "Happee Birthdae Harry" Cake 🚩🚩🚩 72
- Forbidden Forest Cake 🚩🚩🚩🚩🚩 74
- Honeydukes Haul Cake 🚩🚩🚩 78
- Brownie Cauldrons 🚩🚩🚩 80
- Hagrid's Hut Rock Cakes 🚩 82
- Sorting Hat Cupcakes 🚩🚩🚩🚩 84
- House-Elf Carrot Cupcakes 🚩🚩🚩 86
- Hermione's Beaded Bag Cake 🚩🚩🚩🚩 88
- Wizard's Chess Squares 🚩 90
- Hogwarts House Meringues 🚩🚩 92
- Mandrake Bread 🚩🚩🚩🚩 94
- Hogwarts Treacle Tart 🚩🚩🚩 98
- Fluttery Flying Key Cookies 🚩🚩🚩 100
- Monster Book of Monsters 🚩🚩🚩🚩🚩 102
- Dumbledore's Sherbet Lemon Rolls 🚩🚩 106
- Puffskein Cream Puffs 🚩🚩🚩 108
- Knitted Sweater Cookies 🚩🚩🚩 110
- The Burrow Chocolate Cheesecake 🚩🚩🚩 112

TEMPLATES 115
INDEX 122

DIETARY FLAGS

Following a vegetarian, vegan, or gluten-free diet? Look out for these colored flags, as they'll tell you which recipes are suitable for you.

 V — Suitable for VEGETARIANS

 VG — Suitable for VEGANS

 GF — Suitable for those on a GLUTEN-FREE diet

If you are making a vegetarian or vegan bake that requires food coloring, candy, sprinkles, or other store-bought items, always make sure to check the manufacturer's ingredients and select a plant-based option.

Welcome to the Official Harry Potter Baking Book

Go on a magical adventure—every time you step into the kitchen!

From Lightning Bolt Breads, Gryffindor Sword Cookies, and Nimbus 2000 Crackers to Hagrid's Hut Rock Cakes, Nicolas Flamel's Parcels, and Quidditch Pitch Focaccia, this magical book is packed with tasty recipes inspired by the films of Harry Potter.

Before beginning each bake, ensure you have all the ingredients and utensils listed on the page—plus Hermione Granger's eager intellect, Harry Potter's unwavering courage (for the trickier ones), and Ron Weasley's famous love of food! The latter is especially important, as these recipes are all designed to make your mouth water, with lots of healthy ingredients and plenty of vegetarian, vegan, and gluten-free options too (which we've signposted with little colored flags—look out for them).

Also remember to look out for the lightning bolt symbols. They signify the difficulty rating of each recipe, from one bolt (beginner) all the way up to five bolts (complex). You could start with one of the simpler bakes and work your way up—or you could just jump right in. We guess it all depends on whether you see yourself as a Gryffindor, a Slytherin, a Ravenclaw, or a Hufflepuff! (On that note, the Hogwarts Crest Pie on pages 24-25 is simply delicious, as are the Hogwarts House Meringues on pages 92-93.)

Once you've chosen your recipe, remember to wash your hands properly with soap and water and put on an apron to protect your clothes. If you're not yet old enough to practice magic outside the walls of Hogwarts, always make sure you have adult supervision when cooking, especially while using knives and machinery or operating hot ovens and pans. For those with fan-assisted ovens, reduce temperatures by 10-20°C. Please check your manufacturer's handbook or use an oven thermometer. Also, make sure an adult helps you read through the recipes for any allergen concerns.

Finally, grab a pencil (or wand if you have one) and say out loud: "I solemnly swear that I am up to no good!" It'll put you properly in the mood to create some Harry Potter kitchen magic.

KITCHEN SAFETY

The recipes in this book are so tasty, we're sure you'll want to start baking immediately, but before you do, read these top tips for safety in the kitchen. They'll ensure that when you do begin, everything goes magically.

BEFORE

Tip #1

Wash your hands thoroughly with soap and water, then dry them carefully with a clean towel.

Tip #2

Put on an apron to protect your clothes, and if you have long hair, tie it back.

Tip #3

Read through the recipe in advance, making sure you have all the ingredients and utensils you need.

Tip #4

Ensure the area where you'll be working is nice and clean (and keep it that way as much as you can as you go along).

DURING

Tip #5

Ask an adult to help you with anything sharp (like knives) or hot (like ovens).

Just not someone like Gilderoy Lockhart, please —we all remember what happened to poor Harry's arm!

Tip #6

Remember to always wear protective gloves when using the oven, and always chop away from yourself when using knives.

AFTER

Tip #7

Never serve food when it's piping hot. Let it cool slightly before you tuck in.

Your friends aren't dragons, after all!

IMPORTANT!

On occasion, if not handled properly, food can make you unwell, so always wash fruit, vegetables, and herbs before using and keep raw meat and fish away from other foods.

If your chosen recipe does include raw meat, use a separate chopping board for these, if possible. And make sure to wash your hands afterward.

KITCHEN SAFETY

SAVORY

"Let the feast begin!"

PROFESSOR DUMBLEDORE

Savory foods are salty or spicy in flavor.
In this section, you'll bake your way through
some delicious savory dishes.

LIGHTNING BOLT BREADS

 MAKES 8   **20 MINS, PLUS PROOFING**   **12 MINS**

Harry received his lightning bolt scar after a grave encounter with Lord Voldemort when he was just a baby. It is a permanent reminder that he is no ordinary wizard; he is The Boy Who Lived! Create your own version of Harry's iconic mark with these melt-in-your-mouth cheesy flatbreads.

FOR THE BREADS

3 cups/375 g white bread flour

1 tsp active dry yeast

3 tbsp finely chopped fresh herbs, or 1 tsp dried

½ cup/60 g finely grated cheddar cheese

3 tbsp olive oil

1 tsp salt

TO FINISH

4 tbsp finely grated cheddar cheese

Paprika, to sprinkle

 VG Substitute with your favorite vegan cheese for a delicious vegan version.

1. To make the bread, put the flour, yeast, herbs, cheese, oil, and salt in a bowl. Add a scant 1 cup/250 ml warm water and mix well with a round-bladed knife until the mixture comes together to form a dough. Add a little more water if the dough is dry and crumbly.

2. Turn out onto a lightly floured surface and knead for 10 minutes until the dough is completely smooth and elastic. Place in a lightly oiled bowl, cover with plastic wrap, and leave in a warm place for about 1–1½ hours, or until the dough has doubled in size.

3. Preheat the oven to 425°F/220°C/gas mark 7. Line two baking sheets with baking parchment. Turn the dough out onto a lightly floured surface and cut into eight pieces. Roll out each piece to an oval measuring about 6½ x 4½ inches/17 x 11.5 cms.

4. Place four pieces on each baking sheet, spacing them slightly apart. Use the tip of a sharp knife to mark a large scar shape on each.

5. Cover loosely with oiled plastic wrap and leave in a warm place for about 30 minutes, until slightly risen. Bake for 10 minutes. Sprinkle with the cheese and paprika and return to the oven for a few minutes, until the cheese has melted. Serve warm or cold.

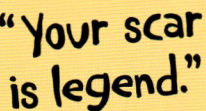

> "Your scar is legend."
> —LUCIUS MALFOY
> *Harry Potter and the Chamber of Secrets*

MAGICAL FACT

Over the course of filming the eight Harry Potter movies, Harry's lightning bolt scar was applied to actor Daniel Radcliffe's forehead more than two thousand times.

BREADS
12

TOP TIP

These breads freeze well if you want to make them ahead of time. Reheat from frozen in a hot oven set to 350°F/180°C/gas mark 4 for 10 minutes.

WAND BREADSTICKS

 MAKES 8   1 HOUR, PLUS PROOFING   10 MINS

Make breadstick wands worthy of Ollivanders wand shop with this tasty bake. But which style to opt for? Hermione's twisting ivy pattern? A tree-trunk handle like Harry's? Or perhaps a unique design of your own? The wand chooses the wizard, after all. Whatever you decide, we guarantee they'll taste amazing ... after you finish waving them. All together now: ⚡Expecto Patronum!⚡

FOR THE WANDS

- 1¼ cups/155 g whole wheat bread flour
- ¼ tsp active dry yeast
- 1 tsp dried mixed herbs
- 1 tbsp olive oil
- ½ tsp salt
- Almond or oat milk, for brushing

FOR THE DIP

- ½ cup/120 g dairy-free yogurt
- ½ cup/120 g vegan mayonnaise
- 2 tbsp vegan black olive tapenade

1. Put the flour, yeast, herbs, oil, and salt in a bowl. Add ⅓ cup/90 ml warm water and mix well with a round-bladed knife until the mixture comes together to form a dough. Add a little more water if the dough is dry and crumbly. Turn out onto a lightly floured surface and knead for 10 minutes, until the dough is completely smooth and elastic. Place in a lightly floured bowl, cover with plastic wrap, and leave in a warm place for 30 minutes.

2. Preheat the oven to 425°F/220°C/gas mark 7. Line a large baking sheet with baking parchment. Turn the dough out onto a lightly floured surface and cut into eight even-sized pieces. Roll each under the palms of your hands to shape wands, making them thicker at the "handle" end and tapering to a point at the other. The dough will expand as it bakes, so roll the wands very thin. Each should be about 12 inches/30 cms long.

3. Brush the wand breadsticks lightly with almond or oat milk and bake for 8–10 minutes, or until firm to the touch.

4. While baking, beat together the yogurt and mayonnaise. Transfer all but a tablespoonful into a serving bowl. Stir the tapenade into this and swirl into the yogurt mayonnaise. Serve with the wands.

PESTO

VEGAN CHEESE DIP

TOMATO SALSA

In addition to our suggestion above, you could also serve your wands with pesto, tomato salsa, or vegan cheese dip. They'll definitely help to cast the right spell.

TOP TIP

Eager to make the wand of your favorite Harry Potter character? Check out our examples and shape your bake accordingly. These have been personalized for Harry, Hermione, Ron, Ginny, and Professor Dumbledore.

Hermione · Ron · Harry · Dumbledore · Ginny

BREADS

Mimbulus Mimbletonia Bagel Loaf

 1 LOAF   **1 HOUR, PLUS PROOFING**   **35 MINS**

If, like Neville, you've been paying close attention in Professor Sprout's Herbology class, you'll know that *Mimbulus mimbletonia* is a rare magical plant that looks a bit like a cactus but with boils instead of spikes. This irresistible recipe shows you how to grow your own. And don't worry, we've left out the Stinksap!

V

FOR THE BREAD
4 cups/500 g white bread flour
1½ tsp active dry yeast
1½ tsp salt
1 large egg, beaten
2 tbsp olive oil
2 tbsp granulated white sugar

TO FINISH
1 large egg white, beaten
Generous ½ cup/150 g basil pesto
½ red pepper

SPECIAL EQUIPMENT
6 cup/1½ liter capacity loaf tin
Pastry brush
Slotted spoon

1 To make the bread, put the flour, yeast, salt, egg, oil, and sugar in a bowl. Add 1 cup/250 ml warm water and mix well until it forms a dough. Add a little more water if the dough is dry and crumbly. Turn out onto a floured surface and knead for 10 minutes, until the dough is completely smooth and elastic. Place in a lightly oiled bowl, cover with plastic wrap, and leave in a warm place for 1–1½ hours, or until the dough has doubled in size.

2 Grease a 6 cup/1½ liter capacity loaf tin. Lightly flour a large baking sheet. Punch the dough to deflate it, and turn out onto a floured surface. Shape the dough into small balls, varying them in size so they are between 1 and 2 inches/2.5 and 5 cms in diameter. Space slightly apart on the baking sheet, cover loosely with a towel, and leave for 15 minutes, until slightly risen. Bring a large saucepan of water to a boil.

3 Carefully transfer a quarter of the dough balls to the boiling water and cook for 1 minute, turning them after 30 seconds. Lift out with a slotted spoon and place on a board. Repeat with the remaining dough balls.

4 Preheat the oven to 425°F/220°C/gas mark 7. Beat the egg white with the pesto in a bowl. Turn one of the dough balls in the pesto so it's generously coated and then place in the tin. Coat another dough ball in pesto and add to the tin. If you find that the dough is patchily covered in the pesto mixture, use a pastry brush to smooth it out. Continue to layer up the dough in the tin, packing the pieces gently together to fit into the corners. Brush any remaining pesto over the top of the dough.

5 Bake the loaf for 30 minutes, covering the bread loosely with foil if it starts to get too brown. Meanwhile, deseed the red pepper and cut into thin ¼ inch/0.5 cm slices. Cut the strips into large tooth-shaped pieces.

6 Remove the bread from the oven and decorate the surface with the pepper pieces. You might find it easiest to make little holes in the surface of the bread with the tip of a sharp knife and push the pepper pieces into the holes. Return to the oven for 10 minutes, covering the loaf loosely with foil if it starts to get too brown. Leave to cool in the tin, and serve warm or cold in chunky slices.

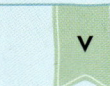

MAGICAL FACT
← When prodded, the *Mimbulus mimbletonia* plant releases a dark green substance from its boils known as Stinksap. As the name suggests, this sap is very, very smelly, so always handle with care.

BREADS

SERVING TIP
This yummy bread is great served as a snack on its own, in sandwiches, or as part of a feast. It can be wrapped in foil and reheated.

Neville can be seen carrying a pulsating *Mimbulus mimbletonia* when the students first arrive at Hogwarts in *Harry Potter and the Order of the Phoenix*. He is later pictured with it again in the Gryffindor common room.

SALAZAR SLYTHERIN'S SOURDOUGH SNAKE

 1 LARGE BREAD   1½ HOURS, PLUS OVERNIGHT STANDING AND PROOFING   30 MINS

One of the most frightful creatures in the Harry Potter movies is the Basilisk, otherwise known as the Serpent of Slytherin. Placed in the Chamber of Secrets by Salazar Slytherin just before he left Hogwarts, this enormous fanged monster is capable of petrifying you with one look. Here, we show you how to make your own ready-to-strike version. Perhaps you'll want to have a Gryffindor Sword Cookie (see pages 66–67) on hand just in case.

1. To make the sourdough starter, put 2 cups/250 g of the flour in a large bowl with the yeast. Add 1 cup/250 ml lukewarm water and mix well to make a thick, sticky batter. Cover the bowl with a dampened towel and leave to stand at room temperature for 24 hours. The batter will rise, and bubbles will form on the surface.

2. The next day, stir in the remaining flour, the salt, and an additional ⅔ cup/150 ml lukewarm water. Mix well to make a soft but not sticky dough. If the mixture is dry and crumbly, add a dash more water. Turn the dough out onto a floured surface and knead for 10 minutes, until smooth and elastic. Transfer to a lightly oiled bowl, cover with plastic wrap, and leave to rise in a warm place until the dough has doubled in size, about 2 hours.

3. Line two baking sheets with baking parchment. Cut a 5 inch/12.5 cm and a 2 inch/5 cm length of cardboard tube and wrap both in foil. Punch the dough to deflate it, and turn out onto a floured surface. Reserve two-fifths of the dough. Roll out the remainder under the palms of your hands until very long, about 40 inches/102 cms, and tapering to a fine point at one end for the tail (see Top Tip).

Continues overleaf.

FOR THE DOUGH
5¼ cups/655 g white bread flour
1 tsp active dry yeast
2 tsp salt

TO FINISH
1 large egg, beaten, to glaze
1 tbsp poppy seeds
Two flaked almonds
Small piece cucumber skin
Green food coloring
Cream cheese (optional)

SPECIAL EQUIPMENT
5 inch/12.5 cm and 2 inch/5 cm diameter cardboard tubes, such as those from a kitchen roll or wrapping paper
Fine paintbrush
Knife (preferably serrated)

 **VG** For a vegan recipe, use oat or rice milk to glaze the bread instead of beaten egg.

TOP TIP When you thinly roll out bread dough, you'll get to a point where the dough becomes so elastic that it won't stretch any more. Simply leave for a few minutes and then roll and stretch the dough again, letting it rest once or twice more if necessary.

BREADS

TOP TIP

The almond "fangs" are quite fiddly to position. To hold them in place, make two slits in the top of the mouth with the tip of a sharp knife and push the fangs in. If they don't sit tightly, use a little cream cheese to secure them.

4 Position the larger wrapped tube upright in the center of one baking sheet. Lift the dough onto the baking sheet and arrange the snake shape, curling the tail end out toward one corner of the baking sheet and loosely wrapping the rest of the dough around the foil tube, making sure the end of the dough finishes behind the tube. Halve the reserved dough.

5 Roll out one piece until about 12 inches/30 cms long and wrap around the tube with the ends again meeting behind the tube. Squash the smaller tube slightly to flatten it and position on the second baking sheet.

6 Roll out the remaining dough until 8 inches/20 cms long and position on the baking sheet with one end of the dough resting on the foil tube to create the curved head. Leave in a warm place covered loosely with oiled plastic wrap for 45 minutes, until risen. Preheat the oven to 425°F/220°C/gas mark 7.

7 Brush the dough with the beaten egg and sprinkle with poppy seeds. Bake for 20 minutes. Remove the head section from the oven and twist out the foil tube from the body. Return to the oven for 10 minutes. Leave to cool.

8 To assemble, with a parent or adult supervision, carefully use a sharp knife, preferably serrated, to cut a small wedge shape from the top of the head to shape the mouth. Push the head piece down into the cavity in the center of the body. Shape and position two pointed fangs from the almonds (see Top Tip) and a long forked tongue from the cucumber skin. Finish by painting eyes using green food coloring.

BREADS

MAGICAL FACT

The Chamber of Secrets was one of the biggest sets created for the Harry Potter movie series, measuring an incredible 250 feet by 115 feet (76 meters by 35 meters). Its deadly resident, the Basilisk, was created using a clever mix of computer effects and animatronics.

BREADS

WIZARDING HATS

 MAKES 10   **20 MINS**   **25 MINS**

These puff pastry and sausage delights are not only easy to make, they're scrumptious too. Which is just as well, because in the wizarding world you're never fully dressed without a hat. This particular style is modeled after Professor McGonagall's pointy black witch's hat, which she is almost never seen without. Do a good job, and you'll definitely earn ten points for your house.

V for a veggie version, use homemade or store-bought vegetarian sausages.

- 1 lb/450 g puff pastry
- 10 breakfast sausages (chipolatas)
- 1 large egg, beaten
- Ground cumin or coriander, to sprinkle

1. Preheat the oven to 400°F/200°C/gas mark 6. Line two baking sheets with baking parchment.

2. Thinly roll out the pastry on a lightly floured surface to an 18 x 13 inch/46 x 33 cm rectangle. Cut in half widthwise. Cut long, pointed triangles from each half so the thick end of each triangle is 4 inches/10 cms wide and the length to the tip is 9 inches/23 cms. Brush the thick ends of each triangle with beaten egg.

3. Using food scissors, cut away the skin from each sausage, keeping the shape intact, and position at the thick end of each triangle. Roll the pastry around the sausage until the sausage is hidden inside the pastry, with ends just sticking out. Pinch the rolled pastry firmly onto the base so it doesn't unravel.

4. Transfer to the baking sheet, spacing the hats slightly apart. Press two folds into each hat and bend the ends to one side to resemble hat shapes.

5. Brush the pastry with plenty of beaten egg and sprinkle lightly with cumin or coriander and a little salt. Bake for 25 minutes, until the pastry is risen and deep golden. Serve warm or cold.

MAGICAL FACT
As well as her pointy black hat, Professor McGonagall also has a tartan deerstalker hat for when she's outdoors. She is seen wearing it during the Quidditch match in the first film.

TOP TIP
Instead of cumin or coriander for sprinkling, try any other favorite flavor, such as paprika, ground chili, curry powder, Moroccan spice, or Za'atar.

INDIVIDUAL BAKES

HOGWARTS CREST PIE

 SERVES 4   1½ HOURS, PLUS CHILLING   45 MINS

Your allegiances will definitely be tested when you dig into this mouthwatering Hogwarts Crest Pie with multiple tasty toppings. Will you opt for a slice of Gryffindor or a slither of Slytherin? Perhaps you fancy a wedge of Ravenclaw or maybe a portion of Hufflepuff? We know what the always-hungry Ron would choose: the lot!

- 1½ lb/675 g puff pastry
- 1 large egg yolk
- Black gel piping pen
- 2 tbsp olive oil, for frying
- 1 large onion, finely chopped
- 1 yellow pepper, finely chopped
- 1 small zucchini/courgette, grated
- ½ cup/120 ml thick tomato sauce
- 1 tbsp basil pesto
- 1 small eggplant/aubergine, finely diced
- 4 cheddar cheese slices
- Salt and pepper, to taste

1. Line two baking sheets with baking parchment. Use paper to trace and cut out all the Hogwarts Crest Pie templates on pages 118–119. Roll out the pastry on a lightly floured surface to ⅛ inch/3 mm thickness and cut around the crest template. Carefully transfer to the baking sheet so the crest doesn't lose its shape. Cut around the remaining templates and place on the other baking sheet. Chill the pastry for at least 20 minutes.

2. Using the tip of a sharp knife, cut a very shallow line ¼ inch/5 mm away from the edges of the crest to create a rim. Cut further double lines ¼ inch/5 mm apart across and down the center of the crest to divide it into quarters, as shown on the template. Brush the rim and central cross with the egg yolk. Brush all over the remaining shapes with egg yolk. Mark shallow, curved cuts on the round shaped part of the crest top (the part that looks like a perfume bottle). Chill the pastry while preparing the filling.

3. Heat two tablespoons of oil in a frying pan and add a third of the onion and the yellow pepper. Cook for 5 minutes. Season lightly with salt and pepper and transfer to a bowl. Add a dash more oil and half the remaining onion and the zucchini to the pan, and fry for 5 minutes. Stir in the pesto and transfer to another bowl. Add a dash more oil and the remaining onion and the eggplant to the pan, and fry until the eggplant begins to caramelize, about 10 minutes.

4. Trace and cut out the animal templates on page 117. Lay them over the cheese slices and cut around with the tip of a sharp knife.

5. Preheat the oven to 425°F/220°C/gas mark 7. Bake the pastry for 10–15 minutes, until risen and golden in color. Using the tip of a sharp knife, lift away the risen centers of the crest and discard, creating cavities for the fillings. Use the black piping pen to write, "*Draco dormiens nunquam titillandus*," onto the thin strip of pastry, and an "H" onto the square section.

6. Pack the fillings into the four crest sections, keeping them neat around the edges. Return to the oven for 6–8 minutes to heat through. Position the cheese shapes and the "H" square and return to the oven for 1 minute to slightly soften the cheese.

7. Transfer to a serving tray/board and position the remaining pastry as shown.

MAGICAL FACT

The Hogwarts motto, which can be seen on the school crest, translates from Latin to "Never tickle a sleeping dragon."

PASTRY

NIMBUS 2000 CRACKERS

MAKES 10 · 30 MINS · 15 MINS

When Professor McGonagall secretly sends Harry a Nimbus 2000 broomstick, he becomes the talk of Hogwarts. It's the latest—and fastest—broomstick on the market, and all his fellow students want one. You too can be the envy of your friends with these bite-sized crackers. Like the Nimbus 2000 itself, they'll be gone before you know it.

V

1. Preheat the oven to 375°F/190°C/gas mark 5. Line a baking sheet with baking parchment. Put the flour, salt, and thyme in a bowl and rub in the butter with your fingertips until the mixture resembles bread crumbs. Stir in the cheese. Put half the egg yolk in a small bowl and add the rest to the dry ingredients. Knead the mixture into a firm dough.

2. Turn the dough out onto a lightly floured surface. Mold into a flat block of dough and roll out to a rectangle measuring 6½ x 5 inches/17 x 12.5 cms. Trim off the raggy edges and cut the dough lengthwise into ten thin strips.

3. Place on the baking sheet, shaping a bend in the center of each and flattening one end with your finger. Stir the chili powder into the reserved egg yolk and brush over the dough. Bake for 15 minutes, or until golden. Cool on the baking sheet.

4. Trim the ends from the scallions and cut lengthwise into thin strips. Once you've separated the scallion layers, you might want to cut the strips into finer lengths. You'll need ten altogether. Pour a little boiling water into a heatproof bowl. Add the scallion strips and soak for 1 minute. Drain.

5. Cut the string cheese into 2 inch/5 cm lengths, then quarter each lengthwise. Separate the strings into as many strands as you can, keeping them intact at one end. Pinch the intact ends flat and rest these over the flattened ends of the sticks. Wrap a scallion strip around each, tie together, and let the ends trail.

- ⅔ cup/85 g all-purpose flour
- Good pinch of salt
- 1 tsp finely chopped thyme
- ½ stick/55 g unsalted butter, firm, diced
- ¼ cup/30 g grated cheddar cheese
- 1 large egg yolk
- ¼ tsp mild chili powder
- 2 scallions/spring onions
- 2 pieces of string cheese

TOP TIP

To shape the bend in your Nimbus 2000 crackers, pinch the dough together gently in the middle with your fingers.

MAGICAL FACT

Harry's Nimbus 2000 was destroyed by the Whomping Willow in *Harry Potter and the Prisoner of Azkaban*, after a Dementor attack caused Harry to fall off the broom midflight.

INDIVIDUAL BAKES

GREAT LAKE TART

 SERVES 6   **50 MINS, PLUS CHILLING**   **1 HOUR**

As the Beauxbatons school champion, Fleur Delacour can be seen at the Great Lake during the Second Task of the Triwizard Tournament. Here, the champions are required to face merpeople and other aquatic creatures as they bid to "recover what we took." Thankfully, you don't have to be a powerful witch to make this scrumptious tart, but you will need roughly an hour for this dish.

FOR THE PASTRY

2¼ cups/280 g all-purpose flour

Good pinch of salt

1½ sticks/165 g unsalted butter, firm, diced

2 large egg yolks

FOR THE FILLING

¼ stick/25 g unsalted butter

1 onion, chopped

8 strips bacon, chopped

2 cloves garlic, crushed

1 cup/175 g frozen sweet corn

3 large eggs

⅔ cup/150 ml heavy cream

⅔ cup/150 ml dairy milk

⅔ cup/75 g grated Stilton or other firm blue cheese

1 large zucchini/courgette

Salt and pepper, to taste

SPECIAL EQUIPMENT

9 inch/23 cm loose-base tart tin

Pie weights/baking beans

 This delicious tart will still have plenty of taste if you simply omit the bacon for a veggie alternative. If you'd like to add another flavor, try a good sprinkling of chopped cilantro/coriander, dill, or chives.

1. To make the pastry, put the flour and salt in a bowl and rub in the butter with your fingertips until the mixture resembles fine bread crumbs. Add the egg yolks and 2 tablespoons of cold water and mix with a round-bladed knife until the dough starts to bind together. Use your hands to bring the mixture into a firm dough. Wrap and chill for 30 minutes.

2. Preheat the oven to 400°F/200°C/gas mark 6. Reserve a quarter of the pastry dough, about the size of a small apple. Thinly roll out the remainder on a lightly floured surface and use to line a 9 inch/23 cm loose-base tart tin. Trim off the excess dough and add this to the reserved dough. Chill the case while preparing the pastry decorations.

3. Trace and cut out the merperson template on page 115. Roll out the reserved pastry and cut around the template. Place on a separate baking sheet lined with baking parchment. Use the tip of a knife to mark the nose. Shape and position lips from the trimmings. From the remaining trimmings, cut plenty of strips as finely as you can with a sharp knife and arrange alongside the face template. Bend some of the strips as you transfer them to the baking sheet, as these will form the creature's hair. Make plenty.

4. Line the pastry case with baking parchment and fill with pie weights/baking beans. Bake the pastry case and decorations for 20 minutes. Remove the decorations from the oven. Remove the paper and beans from the pastry case and bake for 5 more minutes. Reduce the oven to 350°F/180°C/gas mark 4.

5. For the filling, melt the butter in a frying pan and fry the onion and bacon for 5 minutes, until lightly browned. Add the garlic and fry for 2 minutes. Tip into the pastry case and scatter with the sweet corn. Beat the eggs in a bowl with the cream, milk, and a little salt and pepper. Pour over the filling and sprinkle with the cheese. Bake for 20 minutes.

PASTRY

6 Cut thin slices of skin from the zucchini using a small sharp knife. Cut slender leaf shapes from the skin, making them about 1-2 inches/2.5-5 cms long. Arrange around the edges of the tart to represent seaweed. Position the head in the center of the tart and then arrange the hair. Return to the oven for 10-15 minutes, or until the tart is lightly set. While baking, shape two small eyes from the zucchini and position once the tart is baked. Serve warm or cold.

DID YOU KNOW?
Tarts have origins that date back to medieval pie-making. Tarts can be found in early Italian, French, and German cuisine.

MAGICAL FACT
Seen in Harry Potter and the Goblet of Fire (and this bake), merpeople are aquatic beings who inhabit the Great Lake. The film's effects team brought them to life using a combination of computer animation and maquettes.

SAVORY OWL MUFFINS

MAKES 8 | **30 MINS, PLUS COOLING** | **30 MINS**

In addition to being adorable animal companions, owls also deliver mail in the wizarding world—everything from Hogwarts acceptance letters and Firebolt broomsticks to the dreaded Howler (see pages 44–45). Conjure up eight feathered friends with this sumptuous savory bake and then watch them fly—all the way into your mouth!

V | **VG** | **GF**

FOR THE MUFFINS
- 1½ cups/200 g diced sweet potatoes
- 1 cup/125 g gluten-free all-purpose flour
- 3 tbsp cornstarch
- 2 tsp gluten-free baking powder
- 1 tsp baking soda/bicarbonate of soda
- ½ tsp salt
- 3 tbsp chopped chives
- ⅔ cup/150 ml oat milk
- 3 tbsp vegetable oil, plus extra for brushing

TO DECORATE
- ¼ cup/55 g dairy-free spread
- 1 tbsp tomato paste
- Several sliced almonds
- Several radishes
- Several black or red grapes
- Small piece red pepper
- Small piece zucchini/courgette

SPECIAL EQUIPMENT
Muffin tray

1. To make the muffins, preheat the oven to 350°F/180°C/gas mark 4. Brush eight holes of a muffin tray with vegetable oil.

2. Cook the sweet potatoes in boiling water for 10 minutes, until tender. Drain, mash, and leave to cool.

3. Combine the flour, cornstarch, baking powder, baking soda, salt, and chives in a bowl. Stir the milk and vegetable oil into the sweet potato mash until evenly combined. Add to the dry-ingredient bowl and mix well. The consistency should be soft but spoonable.

4. Spoon the mixture into the oiled tray sections and spread level. Bake for about 20 minutes, until risen and firm to the touch. Loosen from the tray and transfer to a wire rack to cool.

5. Beat the dairy-free spread with the tomato paste and spread over the muffins.

6. Arrange overlapping slices of almonds for the feathers. Cut thin slices of radish and position for eyes, adding small pieces of grape for the centers. Cut long diamond shapes from the pepper and position for beaks. Cut thin semicircles of zucchini and position for eyebrows. Store in a cool place until ready to serve.

Give your owls different expressions by moving around their eyebrows. You'll be amazed what a difference the slightest tilt can make.

INDIVIDUAL BAKES

TOP TIP

These little owl faces are best served on the day they're decorated. You can still get ahead by baking the muffins a day in advance, or freezing them, then thawing overnight in the fridge before adding the features.

Pumpkin Patch Pies

MAKES 8   **1 HOUR, PLUS CHILLING**   **40 MINS**

These pumpkin patch pies are so realistic you'll think you're outside Hagrid's hut in the Hogwarts pumpkin patch. Served on a bed of nutritious greens, they're the perfect healthy snack for Halloween—or any other time of year.

1. To make the pastry, put the flour and salt in a food processor and dice in the butter. Blend until the mixture resembles fine bread crumbs. Add 4 tablespoons of cold water and blend again until the mixture forms a dough, adding a dash more water if crumbly and dry. Tip out onto the surface and pat into a neat block. Wrap and chill while preparing the filling.

2. Heat a frying pan and fry the bacon for a few minutes, until beginning to crisp. Add the onion and cook for 3–4 minutes, until softened. Transfer to a bowl and stir in the rosemary or thyme, tomato puree, pumpkin puree, feta, and a little dash of salt and pepper.

3. Cut the celery into 1½ inch/4 cm lengths. Cut each length into thin sticks and place in a bowl of iced water.

4. Preheat the oven to 400°F/200°C/gas mark 6. Line a large baking sheet with baking parchment. Trace the two pumpkin templates on page 116 onto paper and cut out. Cut the dough in half and thinly roll out one half to ⅛ inch/3 mm thickness. Lay the large template over the dough and cut around with a small sharp knife. Cut out as many more pumpkin shapes as you can. Roll out the remaining dough and cut out pumpkin shapes with the smaller template. Reroll the trimmings and cut out more pumpkin shapes until you have an even number of large and small.

5. Brush the edges of half of each size with water and pile the filling into the centers to within ½ inch/1 cm of the edges. Position the remaining pumpkin shapes on top and press down firmly around the edges. Once roughly sealed, lift the pumpkins and pinch around the edges to fully seal. Place on the baking sheet.

6. Add one or two drops of food coloring to the egg yolk and brush over the pastries. Using the tip of a sharp knife, score shallow curved lines over the pastries.

7. Bake the small pastries for about 25 minutes and the large for 35 minutes. Push a piece of celery into the top of each and serve warm or cold on a bed of watercress or pea shoots.

FOR THE PASTRY

2½ cups/315 g all-purpose flour

1 tsp salt

2 sticks/220 g unsalted butter, chilled

FOR THE FILLING

4 strips bacon, chopped

1 onion, chopped

2 tsp finely chopped rosemary or thyme

2 tbsp tomato puree

1½ cups/350 g pumpkin puree

¾ cup/100 g feta cheese, crumbled

TO FINISH

½ celery stick

Few drops natural red food coloring

1 large egg yolk, beaten

Watercress or pea shoots, to serve

Salt and pepper, to taste

V — For a veggie version, omit the bacon and fry a handful of chopped mushrooms in a little oil before adding the onion.

INDIVIDUAL BAKES

NICOLAS FLAMEL'S PARCELS

MAKES 8 • **45 MINS, PLUS CHILLING** • **25 MINS**

Just like the stone itself, there's more to these mouthwatering pastry parcels than meets the eye. Filled with tasty goodness, they won't make you immortal, sadly, but they will delight your tummy. And you don't have to play a life-sized game of wizard's chess or brave Devil's Snare to get your hands on them either.

V | **GF**

FOR THE PASTRY

1¾ cups/250 g gluten-free all-purpose flour

Good pinch of salt

1½ sticks/165 g unsalted butter, firm, diced

1 large egg

FOR THE FILLING

1 tbsp olive oil

2 small onions, finely chopped

2 cloves garlic, crushed

2 tsp cumin seeds

3 tbsp chopped cilantro/coriander

1 cup/160 g cooked chickpeas

1 tbsp clear honey

2 tbsp sun-dried tomato paste

1 cup/150 g grated beets

1 egg, beaten, to glaze

Salt and pepper, to taste

1. Put the flour and salt in a bowl, add the butter, and rub in with your fingertips until the mixture resembles bread crumbs. Add the egg and 1 teaspoon of cold water and mix to a firm dough. Form into a neat, flat block, cover with plastic wrap, and chill for 30 minutes.

2. For the filling, heat the oil in a frying pan and gently fry the onions for 3 minutes to soften. Stir in the garlic, cumin seeds, and cilantro and cook for 1 minute. Tip into a food processor, add the chickpeas, honey, and tomato paste, and blend briefly, until the chickpeas are chopped. Add the beets and briefly blend again until the juice has colored the other ingredients. Season with salt and pepper.

3. Preheat the oven to 375°F/190°C/gas mark 5. Line a baking sheet with baking parchment. Thinly roll out the dough on a lightly floured surface to a rectangle measuring 18 x 9 inches/46 x 23 cms. Trim off any uneven edges and cut out eight 4½ inch/11.5 cm squares. Brush the edges with beaten egg and divide the filling among the centers.

4. Gather up the four corners of one square and pinch together over the filling. Press the edges of the pastry firmly together where they meet. Transfer to the baking sheet and repeat with the remainder. Brush with beaten egg and bake for 20 minutes, until golden. Serve warm or cold.

The only known maker of the stone was alchemist Nicolas Flamel, a long-time friend of Albus Dumbledore's.

MAGICAL FACT

Not only is the stone capable of turning metal into gold, it can also be used to create the Elixir of Life, which makes those who drink it live forever.

INDIVIDUAL BAKES

DEATHLY HALLOWS BREAD

 1 LARGE BREAD 45 MINS 45 MINS

The Deathly Hallows symbol represents the three Hallows: the Elder Wand, the Resurrection Stone, and the Cloak of Invisibility. This bake takes just over an hour from prep to plate. Although it won't make you the master of Death, it will make you the master of your kitchen. Plus, it's hearty and delicious.

FOR THE BREAD

- 2 tbsp olive oil
- 1 large onion, finely chopped
- 2 tsp fennel seeds
- 2 cups/250 g all-purpose whole wheat flour
- 2 cups/250 g all-purpose white flour
- 2 tsp baking powder
- 1 tsp baking soda/bicarbonate of soda
- 1½ tsp salt
- ½ stick/55 g unsalted butter, firm, diced
- 1¼ cups/300 g Greek yogurt
- ½ cup/120 ml dairy milk

TO FINISH

- 2 tbsp olive oil
- 2 green peppers, finely diced
- 5 tbsp black tapenade

SPECIAL EQUIPMENT

12½ x 8¾ inch/32 x 22 cm shallow baking tin or roasting tin

Paper or plastic piping bag

1. Preheat the oven to 425°F/220°C/gas mark 7. Grease the shallow baking tin or roasting tin. Heat the oil in a frying pan and gently fry the onion for 10 minutes, until golden, stirring frequently. Add the fennel seeds and cook for 2 minutes.

2. While frying, put the flours, baking powder, baking soda, and salt in a bowl. Add the butter and rub in with your fingertips. Add the onion mix, yogurt, and milk and mix to a soft dough. Turn out onto a floured surface and roll out until slightly smaller than the dimensions of the tin. Lift into the tin and press the dough firmly down to meet the sides and corners. Bake for 20-25 minutes, until firm and just turning golden. Leave in the tin for 10 minutes, then carefully lift out onto a board.

3. To finish, heat the oil in a frying pan and fry the peppers for about 10 minutes, until softened and beginning to color. Trim off the crusts from the bread and cut the bread diagonally in half. Flip one half over and position against the other half to shape a triangle.

4. Rest a small plate or bowl with a diameter of 7½ inches/19 cms on the center of the triangle and "draw" around with the tip of a sharp knife. Lift away the plate or bowl. Spread 1 tablespoon of the tapenade over the circle and scatter with the peppers, spreading to the edges of the marked circle.

5. Place the remaining tapenade in a piping bag. Snip off the tip so the mixture flows in a fairly thick line. Pipe a line down the center of the bread, then around the edges and finally around the pepper circle.

MAGICAL FACT

The fable of the Three Brothers, and how they came to be in possession of the Deathly Hallows, is recounted by Hermione in *Harry Potter and the Deathly Hallows – Part 1*. She reads the story from the children's book *The Tales of Beedle the Bard*, a favorite of Ron's when he was a little boy.

TOP TIP: If you don't like tapenade, use mayonnaise, tomato paste, or cream cheese for piping. You can also use another color of pepper for the topping.

BREADS

Devil's Snare Pretzel

 1 LOAF   1 HOUR, PLUS PROOFING   40 MINS

In the first film, the dangerous Devil's Snare plant traps Harry, Ron, and Hermione in its tangled tendrils, but they escape its smothering clutches by working together. You and your own best friends can team up to create this brilliant snack, complete with flailing hands for the full awesome effect.

V   **VG**

FOR THE DOUGH

1⅓ cups/200 g diced sweet potato

1 tbsp chopped rosemary

2¾ cups/345 g white bread flour

1¾ cups/220 g whole wheat bread flour

2 tsp active dry yeast

2 tbsp dark brown sugar

1 clove garlic, crushed

1 tsp salt

3 tbsp olive oil

3 tbsp vegan spicy barbecue sauce

1 cup/250 ml warm dairy-free milk

TO FINISH

½ large sweet potato

1 tsp sea salt, plus extra to sprinkle

2 tsp dark brown sugar

Mustard, to serve

SPECIAL EQUIPMENT

Small hand-shaped cookie cutter

1. Cook the sweet potatoes in boiling water for 10 minutes, or until tender. Drain well, mash, and transfer to a large bowl. Add the rosemary, flours, yeast, sugar, garlic, salt, oil, sauce, and all but 2 tablespoons of the milk. Mix to a dough, adding a little more milk if the dough is dry and crumbly. Turn out onto a floured surface and knead for 10 minutes, until smooth and elastic. Transfer to a lightly oiled bowl, cover with plastic wrap, and leave in a warm place until the dough has doubled in size, about 1½ hours.

2. Line a large baking sheet with baking paper. Punch the dough to deflate it, and turn out onto a floured surface. Divide the dough into ten pieces. Roll out two pieces under the palms of your hands until about 30 inches/76 cms long. Twist these together to form a rope and place on the baking sheet in a loose coil. Make two more ropes in the same way and coil over the first, leaving a few gaps through to the baking sheet.

3. Roll the remaining four pieces of dough out as above and coil onto the baking sheet, letting some of the ends trail and curl on the paper to resemble snakes. Cover loosely with oiled plastic wrap and leave in a warm place for 15 minutes, until slightly risen. Preheat the oven to 400°F/200°C/gas mark 6. Cut four thin slices from the sweet potato and stamp out hand shapes using a cookie cutter or by creating a shape of your own.

4. Bake the pretzel for 15 minutes. Combine the salt and sugar in a bowl with 2 teaspoons of boiling water. Brush over the pretzel. Push the potato hands into the bread and return to the oven for 10-15 minutes, until golden. Transfer to a wire rack to cool.

MAGICAL FACT

To defeat the Devil's Snare, Hermione casts *Lumos Solem*, a spell that creates a powerful light. The Devil's Snare hates sunlight! As Harry puts it, "Lucky Hermione pays attention in Herbology."

BREADS

LUMOS SOLEM

DID YOU KNOW?
Pretzels have been around since at least the twelfth century. The earliest documentations of pretzels come from southern Germany and Alsace in eastern France.

DID YOU KNOW? Focaccia is a flatbread that's been around since ancient Rome.

Quidditch Pitch Focaccia

SERVES 12 · **1-1½ HOURS, PLUS PROOFING** · **30 MINS**

In the wizarding world, there's only one sport that gets everyone really excited, and of course it's played on broomsticks: Quidditch. Quidditch is fast, furious, and above all, great fun (unless you get hit by a Bludger, that is). Follow this recipe to create your own Quidditch Pitch Focaccia, complete with six goal posts, two Bludgers, a Quaffle, and the all-important Golden Snitch.

V

1. To make the bread, put the flour, yeast, salt, and 3 tablespoons of the oil in a bowl. Add 1⅓ cups/ 300 ml warm water and mix well with a round-bladed knife until the mixture comes together to form a dough. Add a little more water if the dough is dry and crumbly. Turn out onto a floured surface and knead for 10 minutes, until the dough is completely smooth and elastic. Place in a lightly oiled bowl, cover with plastic wrap, and leave in a warm place for 1 hour, or until the dough has doubled in size.

2. Preheat the oven to 375°F/190°C/gas mark 5. Line two baking sheets with baking parchment. Punch the dough to deflate it. Using a lightly floured hand, pull out a small ball of dough and roll out on a floured surface to ¼ inch/0.5 cm thickness. Place on one baking sheet. Cut out 6 rounds using a 2¼ inch/6 cm cookie cutter.

3. Cut out the centers of the rounds using a 1½ inch/ 4 cm cutter to make hoops. Push the pointed tips of the skewers into one side of each hoop to create lollypop shapes. Bake for 10 minutes until firm. Leave to cool on the baking sheet.

4. Turn the remaining dough out onto a floured surface and roll out to an oval measuring 15 x 11 inches/38 x 28 cms. Transfer to the second baking sheet, making sure the dough keeps its shape. Cover loosely with oiled plastic wrap and leave to rise in a warm place for 30 minutes.

Continues overleaf.

FOR THE BREAD

- 4 cups/500 g white bread flour
- 1½ tsp active dried yeast
- 1½ tsp salt
- 6 tbsp olive oil
- 2 cloves garlic, crushed
- 2 tsp finely chopped rosemary or oregano

TO FINISH

- 1½ cups/340 g cream cheese
- ⅔ cup/40 g finely chopped curly parsley
- Edible liquid gold food coloring
- 2 black olives
- 1 cherry tomato
- Small ball of cheddar cheese, see Snitch Tip (page 42)
- Salt and pepper, to taste

SPECIAL EQUIPMENT

- 2¼ inch/6 cm and 1½ inch/ 4 cm cookie cutters
- Two 7 inch/18 cm bamboo skewers and four 6 inch/ 15 cm bamboo skewers
- Small paper or plastic piping bag

VG For a vegan version, replace cream cheese with your favorite vegan cream cheese and cheddar with your favorite vegan cheddar.

BREADS

5. Mix the remaining olive oil with the garlic, rosemary or oregano, and a little salt and pepper. Push little holes into the surface of the dough with floured fingers and brush the flavored oil over the surface. Bake the dough for 20 minutes, or until pale golden. Leave to cool.

6. Place the focaccia on a serving board. Cover the surface with about two-thirds of the cream cheese, spreading it in an even layer, almost to the edges. Put the remaining cream cheese in a plastic piping bag and snip off the tip. Pipe a line of cream cheese around the edges of the bread and two small curved lines at each end of the bread. Sprinkle the parsley over the central area of the bread, pressing it down firmly in an even layer. Pipe another line across the center of the bread and a final oval shape over this.

7. Paint the bread hoops with gold food coloring and press the three skewers into each end of the dough, with the tallest ones in the center. Scatter the black olive "Bludgers," cherry tomato "Quaffle," and "Golden Snitch" onto the pitch.

SNITCH TIP!

Make your Golden Snitch by finely grating a little cheddar cheese, shaping it into a small, firm ball and rolling it in a little edible gold food coloring. Cut out two wing shapes in thick white paper using the template on page 116. Curl them slightly between your fingers. Push two holes gently into the cheese ball with the tip of a knife and push the wings into the slot.

This bake is a great excuse to play with your food!

BREADS
42

MAGICAL FACT

Like most sports, the aim of Quidditch is to score more points than the opposition, either through goals (worth 10 points) or by catching the Golden Snitch (worth 150 points). Only a Seeker, like Harry, can catch the Golden Snitch, which also signifies the end of the game.

BREADS

Halloumi Howlers

MAKES 8 · **1 HOUR** · **30 MINS**

If there's one thing you don't want to receive in the wizarding world, it's a Howler. These magical letters, which arrive via owl in envelopes, are read out in the sender's voice—usually very loudly indeed. These spinach pastry versions, on the other hand, will be warmly welcomed by the recipient. In fact, you'll likely get an RSVP asking for a second helping.

V

FOR THE FILLING
- 2 tbsp olive oil
- 1 red onion, finely chopped
- 1 stick celery, chopped
- 2 cloves garlic, crushed
- 3 cups/150 g chopped fresh spinach
- 2 cups/200 g grated Halloumi cheese
- 2 tbsp chopped mint
- 2 tbsp chopped dill
- 4 tbsp bread crumbs

FOR THE DOUGH
- 8 sheets filo pastry
- 3 tbsp olive oil
- ½ small eggplant/aubergine
- Dash of black food coloring
- 1 small egg yolk
- Salt and pepper, to taste

SPECIAL EQUIPMENT
Fine paintbrush

1. To make the filling, heat the oil in a frying pan and fry the onion and celery for 3 minutes, to soften. Stir in the garlic and fry for 1 minute. Tip in the spinach and cook for 1-2 minutes, until wilted. Turn into a bowl and add the cheese, mint, dill, bread crumbs, and a little salt and pepper.

2. Preheat the oven to 350°F/180°C/gas mark 4. Line a baking sheet with baking parchment. Trace and cut out the Howler and lip templates on page 116. Place one filo sheet down and brush lightly with oil. Place a second sheet on top. Cut out three 10 x 6 inch/25 x 15 cm rectangles and arrange these with their short sides facing you.

3. Divide the filling mixture into 8 and spoon 3 portions near the top of the 3 rectangles, flattening the filling out to create a rectangle and keeping the mixture ¾ inch/2 cms from the edges.

4. Fold the side edges over the filling and press down gently so the width of the pastries are now about 4½ inches/11.5 cms wide. Fold the top filo edges over the filling. Now fold a rectangle over and along the strip to make a neat rectangle. Repeat with the remainder.

5. Place on the baking sheet with the pastry ends underneath. Make five more parcels in the same way. Brush the tops with oil.

Make sure you stir the filling well so every Howler is equally tasty!

INDIVIDUAL BAKES

6 Layer the remaining pastry until four layers thick and cut around the Howler template. Position over the pastries so the straight-edged tops tuck under the tops of the parcels. Brush these with more oil and bake for 10 minutes.

7 Meanwhile, pare the skin from the eggplant until you have eight pieces, each large enough to cut out a pair of lips using the template as a guide. This is easiest done with a small sharp knife. Beat some black food coloring into the egg yolk.

8 Position the eggplant lips on the parcels and then paint eyes with the egg yolk mixture and a fine paintbrush. Return to the oven for 10–15 minutes, until golden. Serve warm or cold.

DID YOU KNOW?
Halloumi is a kind of cheese that comes from the island of Cyprus, near Greece.

MAGICAL FACT

For the scene in Harry Potter and the Chamber of Secrets where Ron receives a Howler from his mother, actress Julie Walters (who plays Molly Weasley) had to scream so loudly she almost lost her voice.

INDIVIDUAL BAKES

WHOMPING WILLOW CHEESE STRAW

SERVES 6 · **20 MINS** · **45 MINS**

Located on the grounds of Hogwarts, above the entrance to a secret tunnel leading to the Shrieking Shack, the Whomping Willow is a beautiful but violent tree that does not like being disturbed—as Harry, Ron, and Hermione discover on more than one occasion. While the movie version is best avoided, our cheese straw Whomping Willow definitely isn't. With its winding bread branches and parsley leaves, this is a twisty, cheesy treat.

V

- 12 oz/350 g puff pastry
- 1 large egg, beaten, to glaze
- ½ cup/40 g finely grated Parmesan cheese, plus extra to sprinkle
- Plenty of flat-leaf parsley sprigs

1. Preheat the oven to 400°F/200°C/gas mark 6. Line a large baking sheet with baking parchment. Roll out the pastry on a lightly floured surface to a 12 inch/30 cm square. Cut the dough in half and brush one half with beaten egg. Sprinkle with a layer of half the cheese and then place the other half of the pastry on top, sandwiching the cheese.

2. Roll out again to a 17 x 9 inch/43 x 23 cm rectangle and cut lengthwise into 8 thin strips. Brush half the strips with beaten egg and sprinkle with the remaining cheese. Rest the remaining strips on top, pressing them down gently with the rolling pin. Stack 2 of the strips on top of each other and twist together. Repeat with the remainder so you have 2 twisted strips. Transfer to the baking sheet.

3. Create the tree trunk shape by loosely folding one twist over another at the base and then halfway up the pastry, leaving a space in the center to form a hollow in the trunk. Make cuts into the top ends of the pastry strips and open them out—take a little time to arrange the pastry ends into Whomping Willow branch shapes.

4. Brush with beaten egg and bake for 20 minutes. Brush with more beaten egg and sprinkle with a little extra Parmesan.

5. Bake for another 20-25 minutes until the pastry is crisp and golden, covering with foil if the branches start to get too brown. Transfer to a serving board and scatter the branch ends with sprigs of parsley to resemble tree leaves. Scatter more "leaves" around the base of the tree.

MAGICAL FACT

In *Harry Potter and the Chamber of Secrets*, Harry and Ron accidentally crash Arthur Weasley's flying Ford Anglia into the Whomping Willow. To shoot the scene, actors Daniel Radcliffe and Rupert Grint were thrown back and forth in a real car, while mechanical branches "whomped" them. Of course, they had a special stunt team working with them—don't try this at home!

TOP TIP

This is at its best served freshly baked, preferably still warm. You can get ahead by shaping the tree and chilling it on the baking sheet, ready for cooking.

TOP TIP

Try not to move the blueberry slices on the eggs once they're positioned, as they might leave blue marks. You can make the Dark Detectors look more vigilant by varying the positions of the blueberries. Decorate one detector first as a practice to see where you want to position the blueberries.

DID YOU KNOW?

Scones are baked goods that were popularized in Scotland. The first use of the word "scone" dates to the year 1513!

DARK DETECTOR SCONES

MAKES 12 · **40 MINS** · **20 MINS**

A favorite tool of Aurors such as Alastor "Mad-Eye" Moody, Dark Detectors are magical objects capable of telling a good witch or wizard from a bad one (most of the time). Although we can't promise these potato-and-egg-based scones will help you find the Dark wizard in your midst, we can promise you they'll taste incredible.

1. To make the scones, preheat the oven to 400°F/200°C/gas mark 6. Line a baking sheet with baking parchment. Cook the potato in a small saucepan of boiling water for 8–10 minutes, or until tender. Drain, return to the pan, and mash until smooth.

2. Put the flour, baking powder, thyme, and a little salt and pepper in a bowl and rub in the butter with your fingertips. Add the potato and milk and mix with a knife to form a soft dough, adding a dash more milk if the dough is dry and crumbly.

3. Turn out onto a lightly floured surface and roll out to ½ inch/1 cm thickness. Cut out rounds using a 1½ inch/4 cm cookie cutter. Place on the baking sheet and bake for 10 minutes, or until slightly risen and beginning to color. Transfer to a wire rack to cool.

4. Cut a ½ inch/4 cm slice from the center of each egg to leave two domed ends. Beat the mayonnaise in a bowl with a little food coloring until dark gray. Place a small blob on each scone and top with an egg. Put the remaining mayonnaise into a small paper or plastic piping bag and snip off the tip so the mayonnaise can be piped in a thick line.

5. Cut very thin slices from the blueberries and place one on the top of each egg. Pipe a line of mayonnaise on either side of the blueberries to create the eyeball shape. Fill in the areas on either side of the piped line with more mayonnaise. Add small pieces of blueberry to the center of the eyes.

FOR THE SCONES

1 medium potato, peeled and diced

1¼ cups/155 g all-purpose flour

1 tsp baking powder

2 tsp finely chopped thyme

¼ stick/25 g unsalted butter, diced

¼ cup/60 ml dairy milk

TO DECORATE

6 eggs, hard-boiled and shelled

½ cup/120 g mayonnaise

Edible black paste or gel food coloring

Handful of large blueberries

Salt and pepper, to taste

SPECIAL EQUIPMENT

1½ inch/4 cm cookie cutter

Small paper or plastic piping bag

MAGICAL FACT

Dark Detectors don't just root out bad wizards, they also know when a person is telling lies or when something is being concealed.

INDIVIDUAL BAKES

Time-Turner Crackers

 MAKES 10   1 HOUR   10 MINS

These cracker versions of Hermione's time-altering Time-Turner from *Harry Potter and the Prisoner of Azkaban* are easy to make and delicious too. Just make sure you're back where you started (i.e., in a clean and tidy kitchen) before the final chime of the Hogwarts clock tower (or in this case, the oven timer).

V

FOR THE PASTRY

- 1½ cups/190 g all-purpose flour
- ¾ stick/85 g firm unsalted butter, diced
- ½ cup/40 g finely grated Parmesan cheese
- 1 large egg yolk

TO FINISH

- 2 tbsp soft goat cheese
- 20 large green grapes
- 1 tbsp honey
- Potato chips
- Edible gold stars or gold sprinkles
- Edible gold food coloring

SPECIAL EQUIPMENT

- 3¼ inch, 2¾ inch, and 2¼ inch/ 8 cm, 7 cm, and 5.5 cm round cookie cutters
- Small star cutter
- Small paper or plastic piping bag
- Small writer piping tube

1. Preheat the oven to 375°F/190°C/gas mark 5. Line a large baking sheet with baking parchment. Put the flour in a bowl and rub in the butter until the mixture resembles fine bread crumbs. Stir in the cheese. Add the egg yolk and about 1 tablespoon of water, to form a firm dough. Turn out onto a floured surface and knead lightly until smooth.

2. Roll out the dough to a scant ¼ inch/0.5 cm thickness and cut out rounds using a 3¼ inch/8 cm cookie cutter. Transfer to the baking sheet, spacing them slightly apart. Reroll the trimmings to make two more rounds. Cut out two smaller circles from each using 2¾ inch/7 cm and 2¼ inch/5.5 cm cookie cutters. Carefully cut the outer circle of each cracker in half and pull away slightly, without losing the semicircular shape. (Don't worry if some of the semicircular shapes break, as you will only need half of them.)

3. Use the small star cutter to cut out star shapes from the center rounds. Bake the crackers for 10 minutes, until just turning pale golden. Leave to cool on the baking sheet.

4. Put the goat's cheese in a piping bag fitted with a writer tube. Halve the grapes to form half-domes. Secure two of these to each cracker with a dot of the goat's cheese. Sprinkle gold stars or gold sprinkles around the grapes. Brush a little honey over the top of each grape. Pipe a small blob of cheese on the outside of each grape. Pipe two smaller blobs at the inner ends of half the semicircular crackers and rest these gently over each cracker.

5. Paint a little edible gold food coloring over the outer edge of each cracker and over the top edge of the semicircular crackers. Snap the potato chips in half, carve out the middle to create hoop-like shapes, and link these together to resemble a chain from each Time-Turner.

DID YOU KNOW? Hermione's Time-Turner is engraved with the inscription: "I mark the hours, every one, nor have I yet outrun the sun. My use and value, unto you, are gauged by what you have to do."

INDIVIDUAL BAKES

TOP TIP

Decide what you're going to serve the Time-Turners on before you finish decorating them, as it's much easier to arrange the crackers and chains once positioned.

PLATFORM NINE AND THREE-QUARTERS POLENTA BAKE

SERVES 6-8 · 30 MINS · 40 MINS

September 1 marks an important day in the wizarding world. It's when students return to Hogwarts! To get to school, young witches and wizards take the Hogwarts Express at platform nine and three-quarters, which they access through a magical wall. This brilliant recipe shows you how to create your own wall and platform sign. Just don't run into this version!

V · **GF**

FOR THE POLENTA BAKE

- 1 cup/200 g polenta
- 1⅓ cups/190 g gluten-free all-purpose flour
- 2 tsp gluten-free baking powder
- 1 tsp salt
- ½ tsp dried chili flakes
- 4 scallions/spring onions, finely chopped
- 4 tbsp chopped cilantro/coriander
- ½ cup/60 g grated cheddar cheese
- 1 cup/160 g canned or frozen sweet corn
- 3 large eggs, beaten
- ½ cup/120 ml buttermilk
- ⅔ cup/150 ml olive oil

TO FINISH

- 2 slices cheese, e.g., Monterey Jack or cheddar
- ½ cup/65 g gluten-free all-purpose flour
- 2 tsp olive oil
- Natural black food coloring

SPECIAL EQUIPMENT

- 9½ x 7½ inch/24 x 19 cm shallow baking tin or roasting tin
- 2 small paper or plastic piping bags

1. Preheat the oven to 350°F/180°C/gas mark 4. Grease and line a 9½ x 7½ inch/24 x 19 cm shallow baking tin or roasting tin with baking parchment. Combine the polenta, flour, baking powder, salt, chili flakes, scallions, cilantro, cheese, and sweet corn in a bowl. Beat together the eggs, buttermilk, and olive oil and add to the bowl. Stir gently until combined. Turn into the tin and level the surface.

2. Bake for 35-40 minutes until firm to the touch and turning pale golden. Leave in the tin for 10 minutes, then carefully lift out onto a baking sheet.

3. To decorate, cut a 5½ x 2 inch/14 x 5 cm rectangle from the cheese slices and arrange on top of the bread. Mix the flour in a small bowl with the oil and 3½ tablespoons of water to make a loose paste that doesn't quite hold its shape. If a little firm, stir in a dash more water. Transfer a generous tablespoonful of the paste to a separate bowl and add a little black food coloring. Place in a piping bag and snip off the tip so the paste can be piped in a fine line. Use to pipe "9 ¾ Hogwarts Express" onto the cheese.

4. Put the remaining paste into a separate bag and snip off the tip. Use to pipe a line around the edges of the rectangle. Finish by piping a brick design over the surface of the bread. Return to the oven for 3 minutes. Serve warm or cold.

MAGICAL FACT

The cast and crew filmed most of the platform nine and three-quarters scenes at King's Cross railway station in London. However, they used platforms four and five, not nine and ten!

BREADS

Check out the recipe for our Great Hall Chicken Pie on page 56.

Go to page 98 for the lemony Hogwarts Treacle Tart recipe.

These Yorkshire Delights can be found on page 58.

GREAT HALL CHICKEN PIE

SERVES 5-6 · **40 MINS, PLUS CHILLING** · **1½ HOURS**

Prepared by the school's house-elves, meals at Hogwarts are always spectacular, whether it's the start-of-term feast or just an ordinary Tuesday. One dish that always goes down particularly well with students—and teachers!—is a mouthwatering chicken pie. And here's how to make one...

FOR THE FILLING

- 10 boneless, skinned chicken thighs
- ½ stick/55 g unsalted butter
- 1 tbsp vegetable oil
- 2 onions, chopped
- 3 bay leaves
- 2 celery sticks, thinly sliced
- 4 tbsp all-purpose flour
- 2½ cups/600 ml chicken stock
- Small handful tarragon leaves
- 2 cups/200 g sliced mushrooms
- ¼ cup/60 ml heavy cream

TO FINISH

- 1¾ lb/800 g ready-made shortcrust pastry
- 1 large beaten egg, to glaze
- Salt and pepper, to taste

SPECIAL EQUIPMENT

Approximately 9½ inch/24 cm metal pie plate

1. To make the filling, cut the chicken into bite-sized pieces and season with a little salt and pepper. Melt half the butter with the oil in a saucepan and fry the chicken in two batches until lightly browned. Lift out onto a plate. Add the onions, bay leaves, and celery to the pan and fry for 3 minutes.

2. Add the flour, stirring for 2 minutes. Gradually blend in the stock. Return the chicken to the pan with the tarragon and cook gently for 30 minutes. Season to taste.

3. Melt the remaining butter in a frying pan and fry the mushrooms for 5 minutes, until browned. Add to the chicken with the cream and leave to cool. Once cooled, remove the bay leaves.

4. Preheat the oven to 400°F/200°C/gas mark 6. Thinly roll out half the pastry on a lightly floured surface and use to line a 9½ inch/24 cm metal pie plate, so the pastry slightly overhangs the edges. Spoon the filling into the pastry case, doming it up slightly in the center. If there's too much liquid, strain this off and reserve for another use.

5. Thinly roll out the remaining pastry. Dampen the pastry rim with water. Cut the rolled pastry into ¾ inch/2 cm wide strips and use to create a lattice pattern over the pie.

6. Trim off the excess and pinch the pastry around the edges. Brush with beaten egg and bake for about 40 minutes, or until deep golden.

Ron is given a shock, while tucking into his chicken drumsticks, when the ghost Nearly Headless Nick pops up through the table!

PASTRY

MAGICAL FACT

Hogwarts' Great Hall was inspired by two famous real-life halls: the sixteenth-century hall in Christ Church, one of Oxford University's most celebrated colleges, and Westminster Hall in the United Kingdom's Houses of Parliament.

DID YOU KNOW?

In London, England, where Harry finds himself on quite a few occasions, pie shops often sell their pies with jellied eels. Yes, really!

Yorkshire Delights

 MAKES 12   **15 MINS**   **25 MINS**

Yorkshire Delights (called "popovers" in the United States and "puddings" in the United Kingdom) are another firm favorite with Hogwarts students—especially Harry Potter, who absolutely loves them. The key to this recipe is to keep plenty of heat in your muffin pan so that your Delights rise to the occasion. These are best served under thousands of floating candles, with oodles of gravy!

FOR THE MEATBALLS
- 1 cup/225 g lean minced beef
- 1 large shallot, finely chopped
- ½ tsp finely chopped rosemary
- Salt and pepper, to taste
- 2 tbsp light olive oil or vegetable oil

FOR THE BATTER
- 1 cup/125 g all-purpose flour
- ½ tsp salt
- 2 large eggs, beaten
- 1 cup/250 ml dairy milk

SPECIAL EQUIPMENT
12-hole muffin or popover pan, preferably nonstick

1. Preheat the oven to 450°F/230°C/gas mark 8. Thoroughly mix together the lean minced beef, shallot, rosemary, and a little salt and pepper. Roll into twelve even-sized balls.

2. Pour ½ teaspoon of vegetable oil into each section of a twelve-hole muffin or popover pan.

3. Heat in the oven for 5 minutes. Add a meatball to each section and return to the oven for 5 minutes.

4. Meanwhile, make the batter. Put the flour and salt in a bowl, make a well in the center and add the eggs and half the milk. Whisk together, gradually incorporating the flour from around the sides of the bowl until you have a thick, smooth batter. Whisk in the remaining milk and pour into a measuring bowl.

5. Lift the pan from the oven. Working quickly so the oil doesn't cool down, pour the batter into the sections to half fill. Bake for 12-15 minutes, until well risen and golden. Serve warm.

V For a vegetarian option, use your favorite meat-free alternative.

MAGICAL FACT

The design team encouraged the film's young actors to scratch their names and other marks into the four house tables in the Great Hall to make them look older.

INDIVIDUAL BAKES

TOP TIP
These meaty treats make a great lunch or teatime snack as they are, or, for a sweet version, omit the meat and drizzle with maple syrup, chocolate sauce, honey, or fruit puree.

DID YOU KNOW?
These days, a pudding tends to mean a sweet dessert, but hundreds of years ago in Britain, the term was connected to savory and meat-based dishes.

INDIVIDUAL BAKES

DRAGON-ROASTED-NUT TARTS

MAKES 8 | **30 MINS, PLUS CHILLING AND COOLING** | **25 MINS**

Available from a vending machine in Diagon Alley (as seen in *Harry Potter and the Half-Blood Prince*), Weasleys' Dragon Roasted Nuts are a popular snack in the wizarding world—and no wonder! Roasted by an actual dragon (albeit a really tiny one), they bring new meaning to the words "flame grilled." Our version, which can be made in just 30 minutes, even comes with a dragon's nest pastry base to munch on.

- 1 tbsp egg white
- 1 cup/140 g mixed whole nuts, e.g., almonds, hazelnuts, pecans, cashews, walnuts, Brazil nuts
- ½ tsp each of mild chili powder, ground cumin, ground coriander, and turmeric
- ½ tsp salt
- 1 lb/450 g block of puff pastry
- 1 large beaten egg, to glaze
- ¼ cup/60 g mayonnaise
- ¼ cup/60 g Greek yogurt

SPECIAL EQUIPMENT

4½ inch/11.5 cm round cookie cutter
2½ inch/6 cm round cookie cutter
1½ inch/4 cm round cookie cutter

GF For a gluten-free variation of this recipe, you can serve these nuts loose too. Omit the pastry and scatter the spice-coated nuts on a parchment-lined baking sheet. Bake for 10 minutes and leave to cool before serving.

1. Preheat the oven to 425°F/220°C/gas mark 7. Line a baking sheet with baking parchment. Put the egg white in a bowl, add the nuts, and mix well until coated in a thin film of egg white. Sprinkle in the spices and salt and mix again. Scatter onto the baking sheet and bake for 10 minutes. Leave to cool.

2. Roll out the pastry on a lightly floured surface to ⅛ inch/0.2 cm thickness. Cut out rounds using the 4½ inch/11.5 cm cookie cutter. Gently press the 2½ inch/6 cm cookie cutter into the center of each so the cutter leaves an impression but does not cut right through. Use the 1½ inch/4 cm cutter to cut out semicircles from around the edges of the cookies, creating points all around the edge of each pastry. Place on the baking sheet and chill for 20 minutes.

3. Brush the rims of the pastries with the beaten egg and bake for 15 minutes, until risen and golden. Carefully lift away the centers of the pastries to make little containers resembling dragon nests from the First Task in *Harry Potter and the Goblet of Fire*. Leave to cool.

4. Stir together the mayonnaise and yogurt and spoon a little into the base of each tart. Scatter the nuts on top and keep in a cool place until ready to serve.

TOP TIP

There will be quite a few pastry trimmings from this recipe. To avoid wasting them, cut roughly into semicircles to match those already made and mix in a bowl with a little leftover beaten egg, 2 tablespoons of granulated white sugar, and a scant 1 teaspoon of ground cinnamon. Scrunch into little bundles on a baking sheet and bake until golden, then enjoy.

SWEET

"Anything off the trolley, dears?"
"We'll take the lot!"

Trolley Witch and Harry Potter

Sweet foods are, well . . . sweet!
In this section, you'll get your sweet tooth on
as you make your way through some
mouthwatering bakes.

Luna's Spectrespecs Cookies

🍽 MAKES 12   🕐 1 HOUR, PLUS CHILLING   🔥 10 MINS

Modeled by Luna Lovegood in *Harry Potter and the Half-Blood Prince*, Spectrespecs are colorful spectacles that allow the wearer to see Wrackspurts: invisible creatures that float in your ears and make your brain go fuzzy. The only thing these yummy cookies will make go fuzzy are your taste buds—with tingly delight. Enjoy with tea and your favorite magazine (we recommend *The Quibbler*).

FOR THE COOKIES

2⅓ cups/290 g all-purpose flour

1¾ sticks/200 g unsalted butter, firm

¾ cup/100 g confectioners'/icing sugar

2 large egg yolks

2 tsp vanilla extract

12 pink and 12 blue hard candies/boiled sweets

FOR THE FROSTING

1 medium egg white

1½ cups/190 g confectioners'/icing sugar

Pink food coloring

Edible pink glitter, to sprinkle

1. Put the flour in a food processor and dice in the butter. Blend until the mixture resembles fine bread crumbs. Add the sugar and blend briefly to mix. Add the egg yolks and vanilla and blend to a smooth dough. Wrap in plastic wrap and chill for about an hour, until firm.

2. Preheat the oven to 375°F/190°C/gas mark 5. Line two baking sheets with baking parchment. Use paper to trace and cut out the Luna's Spectrespecs template on page 117. Roll out half the dough on a lightly floured surface to ⅛ inch/3 mm thickness, reserving the remaining dough in the fridge. Slide onto one baking sheet.

3. Place the template over the pastry and cut out the specs shape using a small kitchen knife, not forgetting to cut out the center circles. Cut out as many more shapes as you can fit on the dough. Carefully lift away the dough trimmings and chill these. Roll out and cut shapes from the reserved dough and trimmings until you have twelve pairs of specs.

4. Bake the cookies for 5 minutes. Unwrap the candies and place one of each color in each pair of specs. Return to the oven for 5 minutes, or until they've melted to fill the space. If there are any areas where the candies have not completely flooded the space, use a toothpick to push the hot syrup to the edges. Leave to cool completely.

5. Using a whisk, beat together the egg white and confectioners' sugar in a bowl, adding a dash of pink coloring. The mixture should thickly coat the back of a spoon. If too thick, beat in a drop of water. Use a fine brush to spread the frosting over the specs. Leave for a couple of hours, or overnight to set. Serve sprinkled with edible glitter.

> "You're just as sane as I am."
> —Luna Lovegood
> *Harry Potter and the Order of the Phoenix*

TOP TIP

If you have a 1½ inch/4 cm round cookie cutter, use this as a speedy way of cutting out the specs centers.

Gryffindor Sword Cookies

🍽 MAKES 12-14   ⏱ 1½ HOURS, PLUS SETTING   🔥 20 MINS

Channel your inner hero with these *sharply* satisfying cookie replicas of Godric Gryffindor's magical sword. Used by Harry to defeat the dreaded Basilisk and by Ron to destroy the Locket of Slytherin, this ancient blade is one of the most powerful objects in the wizarding world and always appears when you need it most (hopefully including when hunger strikes).

V

FOR THE COOKIES

1 stick/110 g unsalted butter, very soft

½ cup/65 g confectioners'/icing sugar

1 tsp almond extract

1 cup/125 g all-purpose flour

3 tbsp ground almonds

TO DECORATE

1 large egg white

1¼ cups/155 g confectioners'/icing sugar

A little natural black food coloring

About 10 glacé/candied cherries

Tube of gray or black writer frosting

SPECIAL EQUIPMENT

½ inch/1 cm plain piping tube

Large piping bag

1. Preheat the oven to 325°F/160°C/gas mark 3. Trace and cut out the sword template on page 115. Line two baking sheets with baking parchment. Slide the template under the parchment for piping over.

2. Beat together the butter and sugar until very pale and creamy. Beat in the almond extract, flour, and almonds until smooth. Transfer the mixture to a large piping bag fitted with a ½ inch/1 cm plain piping tube.

3. Pipe over the sword template. Start at the handle end, filling in the shape almost to the edges and piping the paste in one long line for the blade. Lift the tube away and pinch the paste to a pointed tip at the end. Slide the template over to another area of the parchment and pipe another sword. Repeat to make 12-14 swords.

4. Bake for 20 minutes, until pale golden. Leave on the baking sheet for 5 minutes, then carefully transfer to a wire rack to finish cooling.

5. To make the frosting, beat together the egg white and confectioners' sugar until smooth and thickly coating the back of the spoon. Beat in a little black food coloring to color the frosting pale gray. Slide a sheet of parchment under the wire rack to catch the drips. Use a pastry brush to coat the cookies in a thin layer of the frosting.

6. While the frosting is still soft, cut small pieces of glacé/candied cherries and use to decorate the handle ends. Leave to set for about 1 hour.

7. To finish decorating, use the tube of writer frosting to pipe decorative lines over the handles of the cookies and a straight line down the centers of the blades.

MAGICAL FACT

When designing the Sword of Gryffindor, the Harry Potter prop-making team sought inspiration from real-life medieval swords. The large rubies on the sword's handle were added to symbolize Gryffindor house.

COOKIES

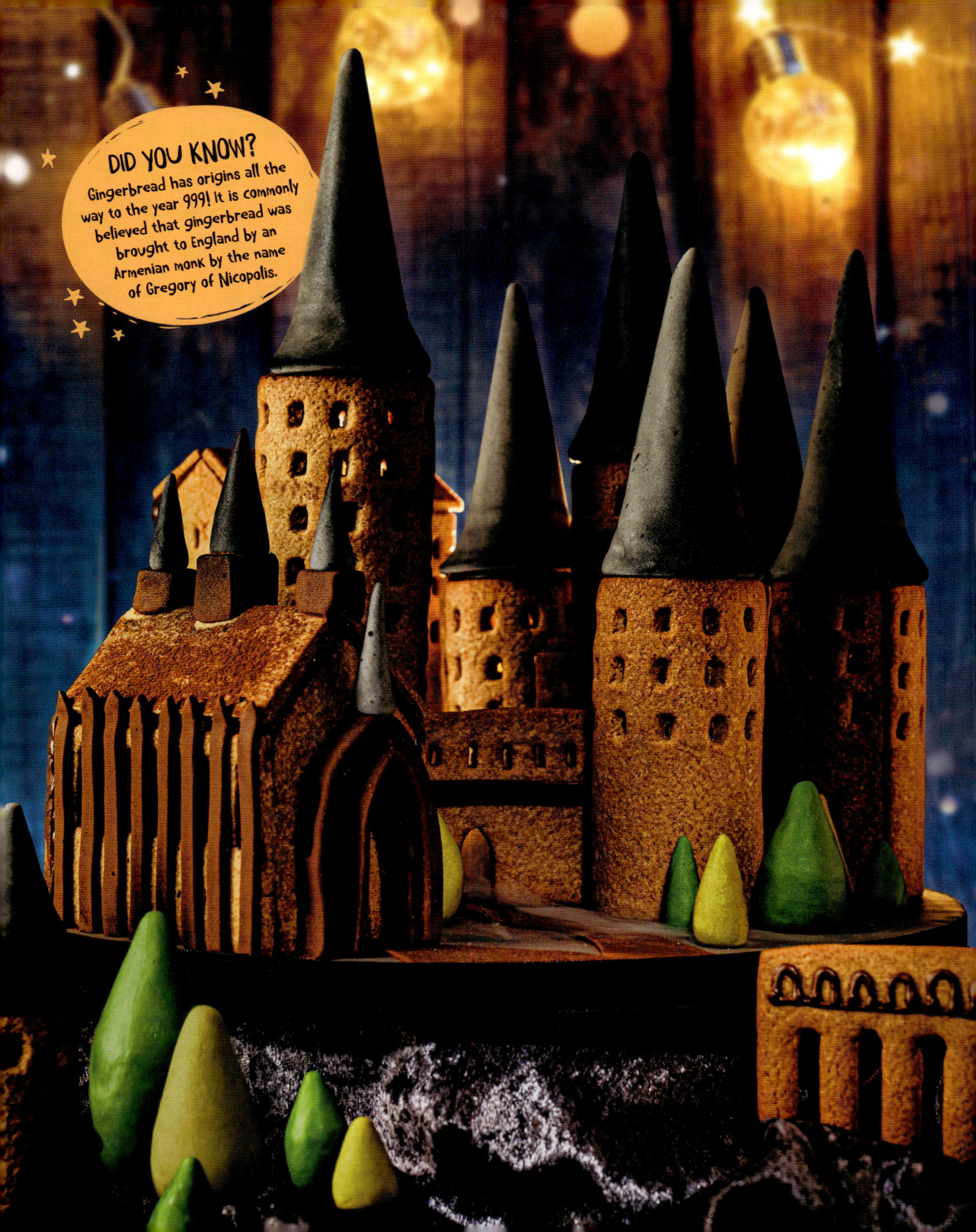

DID YOU KNOW? Gingerbread has origins all the way to the year 999! It is commonly believed that gingerbread was brought to England by an Armenian monk by the name of Gregory of Nicopolis.

Hogwarts Gingerbread Castle

SERVES 28 • **4 HOURS, PLUS CHILLING** • **ABOUT 30 MINS**

Founded more than one thousand years ago by the four most esteemed witches and wizards of the age, Hogwarts School of Witchcraft and Wizardry is the finest school of magic in the world. And now you can create your very own. It may not have 142 moving staircases or a nearly headless ghost, but it does have a magnificent Great Hall. And it's every bit as delicious as it looks.

1. Make each quantity of gingerbread as follows: put the flour, salt, and spices in a food processor. Dice in the butter and blend until the mixture resembles fine bread crumbs. Briefly blend in the sugar. Add the corn syrup, egg, and egg yolk and blend to a smooth, firm dough.

2. Turn out onto a lightly floured surface, pat into a 1 inch/2.5 cm thick block, and wrap in plastic wrap. Make two more quantities in the same way. Chill for a couple of hours or overnight.

3. Use paper to trace and cut out the gingerbread castle templates on pages 120-121, writing on each template the name of the building and number of pieces required. Cut one cardboard tube to 8 inches/20 cms in length, one to 2½ inches/6 cms in length and the remainder to 5 inches/13 cms in length. Wrap each in tin foil, pushing the foil ends neatly down into the tubes. Carefully cut each tube in half lengthwise.

4. Preheat oven to 350°F/180°C/gas mark 4. Line several baking sheets with baking parchment. Thinly roll out one quantity of gingerbread dough on a floured surface to ⅛ inch/3 mm thickness. Lay the templates on top and cut around them with a small sharp knife. Transfer to the baking sheet, spacing the pieces slightly apart and intact.

5. For the towers, thinly roll out more dough and cut out rectangles that are slightly shorter than the foil-wrapped tubes and 3 inches/7.5 cms wide. Use a teaspoon handle to press rows of windows into all the tower pieces. Position the rectangles over the foil tubes and space slightly apart on a baking sheet. Press more windows into the remaining gingerbread shapes, as shown on the templates. Cut out the Great Hall windows with a knife.

Continues overleaf.

---

3 quantities gingerbread dough, see below

1½ lb/675 g gray fondant

Confectioners'/icing sugar and cocoa powder, for dusting

1½ cups/225 g chopped milk chocolate

7 oz/200 g brown fondant

7 oz/200 g green fondant, preferably in two shades

6 ice-cream cones

Edible black food spray, optional

GINGERBREAD

2¾ cups/345 g all-purpose flour

Good pinch of salt

2 tsp ground ginger

2 tsp ground cinnamon

1⅛ stick/125 g firm unsalted butter

1 cup/220 g light brown sugar

4 tbsp corn syrup

1 large egg

1 large egg yolk

You'll need some extra equipment for this recipe.

SPECIAL EQUIPMENT

14 inch/35.5 cm round cake drum

6-8 battery-powered tea lights

Six 2 inch/5 cm diameter cardboard tubes, such as those from a kitchen roll or wrapping paper

Small paper or plastic piping bag

TOP TIP

Make sure the gingerbread dough is very chilled when rolling out. This will make cutting out easier and the pieces will hold their shapes. If the dough softens as you work, rechill it to firm up.

BIG CAKES

TOP TIP
The melted chocolate will gradually solidify in the piping bag. Simply pop it back in the microwave for a few seconds to melt it again if necessary.

6. Bake all the gingerbread pieces, two sheets at a time, for 15-18 minutes, until pale golden. Leave on the baking sheets for 5 minutes. When cool, carefully ease the foil tubes away from the curved pieces of gingerbread.

7. Brush the cake drum lightly with water. Roll out 8 oz/225 g of the gray fondant very thinly on a surface dusted with confectioners' sugar. Lift onto the cake drum board and roll the fondant right to the edges so the board is covered. Trim excess fondant.

8. Melt the chocolate and transfer to a small paper piping bag. (Keep the remaining chocolate for later.) Snip off the tip so the chocolate can be piped in a thin line. Cool for a few minutes.

9. Gently secure the front piece of the Great Hall and one long side together with piped chocolate so that the pieces hold together. (You might need to prop them up with cans until the chocolate sets.) Secure the second long side in place and then the back. Pipe more chocolate along the top edges and position the roof sections. Use this method to secure the Astronomy Tower base and School of Witchcraft and Wizardry together.

10. Assemble all the curved gingerbread sections together in pairs using more piped chocolate, to create the towers. Position the Great Hall at one edge of the board and the tallest tower next to it. Secure the archway next to the tall tower and then the tower base next to this. Position the four medium-sized towers at the corners of the tower base building and then the smallest tower on top of the base. Place the School of Witchcraft and Wizardry building at the back of the board. Once you're happy with the positioning, secure all the buildings except the Great Hall and School of Witchcraft and Wizardry to the fondant base with more melted chocolate.

MAGICAL FACT
Hogwarts Castle was inspired by two of the United Kingdom's most famous universities: Oxford and Cambridge.

Festive Hogwarts

If you like, add further decorations such as a Hogwarts Castle bridge, made from gingerbread dough trimmings, another small tower, and several trees. Try dusting the peaks of the castle with confectioners' sugar to give the effect of snowfall on the roof.

11 Roll out the brown fondant and cut eight 3¼ x ¼ inch/8 x 0.5 cm lengths. Shape points at one end and secure to the long outside wall of the Great Hall with melted chocolate. Shape more brown fondant into the square bases for the Great Hall roof turrets, a footpath at the front of the castle, and decorations over the arch. Use the remainder to shape the front of the Great Hall and secure in place with melted chocolate.

12 Roll out a little gray fondant, brush lightly with water, and wrap around an ice-cream cone, smoothing to fit. Trim off excess fondant at the base and position on one of the towers. Shape and position the remainder in the same way. Use the fondant trimmings to shape small turrets for the Great Hall. Secure the turrets in place with chocolate in those that you're not going to be placing tea lights in. If you like, lightly spray the turrets with edible black food spray.

13 Use the green fondant to shape a selection of small trees and place these around the board. Dust the tops of the pitched roof buildings with cocoa powder. Carefully lift the two pitched roof buildings and position two tea lights under each. Position more tea lights in several of the towers and tucked around the back of the arch.

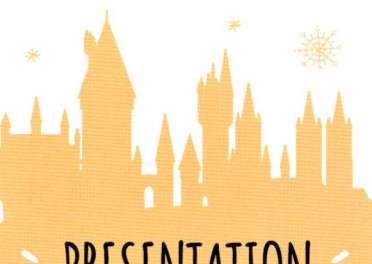

Presentation

To make your castle look really effective and give it stature, raise it up on a fabric-draped base. Use a large, deep upturned bowl or a stack of books or magazines. Position a round cake board on top and drape the fabric or crumpled paper over this. Position the gingerbread castle and secure a black ribbon around the edges of the silver board.

BIG CAKES

"Happee Birthdae Harry" Cake

SERVES 12 · **1¼ HOURS, PLUS COOLING** · **25 MINS**

Make someone's big day extra special with this "Happee Birthdae Harry" Cake. An exact replica of the one Hagrid gave to Harry on his eleventh birthday (although not quite as squashed hopefully), it's the perfect treat for wannabe wizards and witches everywhere. Try not to break any doors down when you deliver it, though!

V · **VG**

FOR THE CAKE
- Dairy-free spread, for greasing
- 3 cups/375 g all-purpose flour
- 1½ cups/300 g granulated white sugar
- 6 tbsp cocoa powder
- 2 tsp baking soda/bicarbonate of soda
- 1 tbsp white wine vinegar
- 1 tbsp vanilla extract
- 1 cup/250 ml dairy-free milk
- 3.5 oz/100 g vegan chocolate

TO DECORATE
- Small bunch of beets
- 3.5 oz/100 g block creamed coconut, chopped
- ½ cup/120 ml dairy-free milk
- 2 tsp vanilla extract
- 4⅓ cups/550 g confectioners'/icing sugar
- 1 tbsp cocoa powder
- Vegan green food coloring

SPECIAL EQUIPMENT
- Small paper or plastic piping bag
- Two 8 inch/20 cm loose-base cake/sandwich tins

1. Preheat the oven to 375°F/190°C/gas mark 5. Grease two 8 inch/20 cm loose-base sandwich tins and line the bases with baking parchment. Put the flour, sugar, cocoa powder, and baking soda in a large bowl. Stir in the vinegar, vanilla, and milk and beat until smooth, creamy, and slightly paler in color. Stir in the chocolate. Divide between the tins and level the surfaces.

2. Bake for 25 minutes, until just firm to touch. Loosen the edges and transfer the cakes to a wire rack to cool.

3. Finely grate the beets into a bowl. Tip out onto a double thickness of kitchen paper. Bring the edges of the paper up around the beets. Hold the parcel over a bowl and squeeze to remove as much juice as possible.

4. Put the coconut and milk in a small saucepan and heat gently, until the coconut has melted. Transfer to a large bowl and add the vanilla and sugar. Whisk well to make a thick, smooth frosting with a spreadable consistency. If too thick to spread, add a dash more milk; if too thin, a little more confectioners' sugar.

5. Transfer a generous third of the mixture to a separate bowl and stir in the cocoa powder. Use this to sandwich the cakes together on a serving plate. Transfer another 2 tablespoons of the frosting to a small bowl and stir in a dash of green food coloring. Place in a small plastic or paper piping bag.

6. Beat 1 teaspoon of the beet juice into the remaining frosting. Gradually add more beet juice, drop by drop, until the frosting is deep pink. Spread this over the top and sides of the cake, spreading the frosting as smoothly as possible using a spatula.

7. Snip the smallest tip off the piping bag so the frosting can be piped in a fine line. Use to write "Happee Birthdae Harry" onto the top of the cake. Store in a cool place until ready to serve.

TOP TIPS — This cake can be made and decorated a day in advance. You can also personalize it to you by swapping "HARRY" for another name.

JUST DON'T SIT ON IT LIKE HAGRID DID!

BIG CAKES

FORBIDDEN FOREST CAKE

SERVES 12 | **2 HOURS, PLUS COOLING** | **25 MINS**

Hogwarts' Forbidden Forest is off-limits to students for a reason: It's home to Aragog the Acromantula and his many hungry children. With Hagrid's giant, eight-legged friend perched on top, this chocolate cake may look a bit frightening, but it tastes anything but. Even Ron, with his deathly fear of spiders, wouldn't say no to a second helping.

GF **V**

1. To make the sponge, preheat the oven to 350°F/180°C/gas mark 4. Grease the base and sides of three 7 inch/18 cm sandwich tins and line the bases with baking parchment. Beat together the butter and sugar in a large bowl until pale and creamy. Gradually beat in the eggs a little at a time, spooning in a little of the flour if the mixture starts to separate.

2. Stir in the vanilla, then sift in the flour, baking powder, and cocoa powder. Fold in until combined, then gently stir in the milk.

3. Divide among the tins, level the surface, and bake for 25 minutes, or until just firm to the touch. Transfer to a wire rack to cool.

4. For the frosting, put the chocolate chips in a bowl. Heat the cream in a saucepan until bubbling up around the edges but not boiling. Pour over the chocolate chips and leave until the chocolate has melted, stirring frequently until smooth. Once cool, chill in the fridge for at least 2 hours, until firm enough to spread but not set.

5. To assemble the cake, cut out the center of one of the cake layers. This is easiest done by placing a 5½ inch/14 cm plate or bowl over the cake and cutting around it with a sharp knife, making sure you keep the knife completely vertical. Carefully lift out the center and reserve.

6. Place another cake layer on a serving board or plate that's at least 4 inches/10 cms wider than the cake. Spread the top edges with a little frosting. Carefully lift the hollowed-out cake layer on top. Scatter the jelly candies into the cake cavity in an even layer. Spread a little more frosting over the cake rim and position the top layer.

7. Crumble the reserved cake sponge into a bowl. Add enough of the frosting, about 4 tablespoons, to make the crumbs bind together. Set aside to use in step 9. Spread the remaining frosting over the top and sides of the cake, and around the edges of the board, with a spatula.

Continues overleaf.

FOR THE SPONGE

2½ sticks/275 g unsalted butter, softened, plus extra to grease

1⅓ cups/300 g light brown sugar

5 large eggs, beaten

2 cups/250 g gluten-free all-purpose flour

1 tbsp vanilla extract

2 tsp gluten-free baking powder

¼ cup/30 g cocoa powder

4 tbsp dairy milk

CHOCOLATE FROSTING

2 cups/300 g milk chocolate chips

1⅓ cups/300 ml heavy cream

TO FINISH

2 cups/250 g insect-shaped candies/sweets, e.g., jelly slugs, worms, or snakes

⅔ cup/60 g gluten-free white marshmallows

1 stick soft black licorice

¼ cup/40 g dark chocolate chips

SPECIAL EQUIPMENT

Small paper or plastic piping bag

Three 7 inch/18 cm sandwich tins

BIG CAKES

TOP TIP

To melt chocolate, place the chocolate chips in a heatproof bowl and rest it over a small pan of simmering water until melted. Alternatively, microwave on medium power, in short spurts, stirring frequently until smooth.

PRESENTATION

The marshmallows make a really effective spiderweb! If the mixture starts to set before you've finished making the web, heat it again—but very gently, as it will start to toast. Once you've finished with the pan, leave it to soak in cold water so it's easy to clean.

8 Put the marshmallows in a small saucepan and heat gently, stirring occasionally, until the marshmallows have melted. Leave to stand for a few minutes, until cool enough to handle with your fingers. Take a little of the mallow mixture between your fingers and pull it apart into thin strands. Drape this over one side of the cake to create a spiderweb effect. Repeat several times.

9 For the spider, roll a walnut-sized piece of the cake crumbs and position on the web, adding a smaller piece for the face. Cut the piece of licorice to 3½ inches/9 cms. Cut eight thin lengthwise strips from the licorice for the legs. Pinch one strip firmly between your finger and thumb, about a third of the way along the licorice to shape a bent leg. Secure to the spider's body and position seven more legs in the same way.

10 From the remaining cake crumbs, shape plenty of treelike roots, tapering each to a point at one end. Secure the thick ends to the sides of the cake and let the tapered ends trail over the board.

11 Melt the chocolate and place in a small paper or plastic piping bag. Snip off a small tip so the chocolate can be piped in a thin line. Use to pipe the spider's eyes and then plenty more trailing tree roots around the sides of the cake.

MAGICAL FACTS

Fully grown Acromantulas can grow to the size of elephants, as Harry and Ron discover to their horror when they meet Hagrid's spider friend Aragog and his family for the first time in *Harry Potter and the Chamber of Secrets*. Rather than using visual effects, the Harry Potter creature shop built a life-sized mechanical model of Aragog, using a system called aquatronics to make its movements look realistic.

As well as Aragog and his family, the Forbidden Forest is home to Thestrals, Unicorns, and Centaurs (like these ones).

BIG CAKES

HONEYDUKES HAUL CAKE

 MAKES 16   1 HOUR, PLUS PROOFING AND COOLING   12 MINS

There are lots of places we'd love to visit in the wizarding world, but Honeydukes Sweet Shop in Hogsmeade is top of the list. Home to every type of sweet imaginable, from Chocolate Frogs to Bertie Bott's Every-Flavor Beans, it's the stuff dreams are made of—and the inspiration for this incredible, candy-covered doughnut cake. (We've left out the earwax-flavored ones, we promise!)

FOR THE DOUGHNUTS

4 cups/500 g white bread flour

½ stick/55 g unsalted butter, firm, diced

2 tsp active dry yeast

1 tsp salt

⅓ cup/70 g granulated white sugar

2 tsp vanilla extract

1 cup/250 ml warm milk, plus 1 tbsp

TO FINISH

⅓ cup/110 g strawberry or raspberry jam

4 tbsp confectioners'/icing sugar

½ tsp ground cinnamon

⅔ cup/135 g granulated white sugar

Selection of candies/sweets, e.g., jelly beans, Acid Pops, Chocolate Frogs, sherbet lemons

Pink sugar sprinkles

Gold or silver stars, or edible glitter

SPECIAL EQUIPMENT

¼ inch/0.5 cm plain piping tube

Paper or plastic piping bag

1 To make the doughnuts, put the flour and butter in a bowl and rub in with your fingertips. Add the yeast, salt, sugar, vanilla, and milk and mix to a soft but not sticky dough, adding a dash more milk if the dough is dry and crumbly.

2 Turn out onto a floured surface and knead for 10 minutes, until smooth and elastic. Transfer to a lightly oiled bowl, cover with plastic wrap, and leave to rise in a warm place, until the dough has doubled in size, about 1½ hours.

3 Line two baking sheets with baking parchment. Punch the dough to deflate it, and turn out onto a floured surface. Cut into 16 even-sized wedges and shape each into a ball. Space apart on the baking sheets, cover with lightly oiled plastic wrap, and leave in a warm place until doubled in size, about 1¼ hours. Preheat the oven to 375°F/190°C/gas mark 5.

4 Bake the doughnuts for about 12 minutes, until risen and golden. While baking, put the jam in a plastic piping bag fitted with a ¼ inch/0.5 cm plain piping tube. Mix the confectioners' sugar in a bowl with 2 tablespoons of water to make a thin glaze. Mix together the cinnamon and sugar on a plate.

5 Make a small hole on one side of each doughnut and squeeze in a little jam. Brush the doughnuts with the sugar glaze and roll in the cinnamon sugar. Pile up on a serving plate or cake stand.

6 To serve, scatter the candies around the base and in between the doughnuts. Sprinkle with the pink sugar and stars or glitter.

MAGICAL FACT

Professor Dumbledore is very unlucky when it comes to Bertie Bott's Every-Flavor Beans. He had a vomit-flavored one as a boy, and in the first film, he chooses what he thinks is toffee, but it's actually earwax!

BIG CAKES

TOP TIP

The doughnuts can be made, filled, and sugar-dusted a day in advance and stored in an airtight container. Assemble up to a few hours before serving.

BROWNIE CAULDRONS

MAKES 6 · **1-1½ HOURS, PLUS COOLING** · **20 MINS**

Cauldrons are used in the wizarding world to brew all kinds of spells, from Felix Felicis (better known as Liquid Luck) to Polyjuice Potion. They're on the list of requirements for all first-year Hogwarts students, and this sumptuous recipe shows you how to make your own delicious brownie versions, plus some for your friends.

V · **VG**

FOR THE BROWNIES
- 5 tbsp vegetable oil, plus extra to grease
- 1 cup/200 g chopped plain or milk vegan chocolate
- 1¼ cups/155 g all-purpose flour
- 3 tbsp cocoa powder
- ¾ cup/170 g light brown sugar
- ⅔ cup/100 g finely chopped pecans or walnuts
- 1 cup/250 ml dairy-free milk
- ¾ cup/200 g vegan chocolate spread

TO DECORATE
- ¼ cup/50 g dairy-free spread
- 1 cup/125 g confectioners'/icing sugar
- Green, black, and purple natural food coloring
- 2 oz/50 g brown fondant
- 3 tbsp granulated white sugar

SPECIAL EQUIPMENT
- Twelve 2¾ inch/7 cm spherical baking molds
- Palette knife

Hermione brews the complicated Polyjuice Potion in her second year at Hogwarts.

1. Preheat the oven to 350°F/180°C/gas mark 4. Cut out twelve 2¼ inch/6 cm circles of baking parchment and snip all around the edges. Lightly oil twelve 2¾ inch/7 cm spherical baking molds and press a parchment circle into each to line the bases. Melt the chocolate.

2. Combine the flour, cocoa powder, sugar, and nuts in a bowl. Mix together the milk and remaining oil and add to the bowl with the melted chocolate. Stir until combined, then divide among the molds and spread level. Place on a baking sheet and bake for 20 minutes, until slightly risen and firm to the touch. Leave in the molds to cool.

3. Carefully loosen the molds with a knife and turn out the cakes. Slice off any domed surfaces of the cakes and sandwich in pairs with a little of the chocolate spread to create spheres. Cut a thin slice off the top of each.

4. Using a small palette knife, spread a thin layer of chocolate spread over the sides of the cakes, spreading it as smoothly as possible.

5. To decorate, put the dairy-free spread and confectioners' sugar in a bowl and beat until smooth and creamy. Transfer a third to a separate bowl. Beat a little green food coloring into the larger quantity and purple into the other.

6. Take six small pieces of the brown fondant and roll out each under the palms of your hands until about 5 inch/13 cm long. Position around the top of each cake to form a rim, pressing the ends gently together.

7. Spoon a little of the green frosting onto each cauldron and spread to the rims with the back of a teaspoon. Spoon a little purple frosting on top.

8. Put the sugar in a small bowl with a little purple food coloring and work the color into the sugar with the back of a teaspoon. Sprinkle a little over the cauldrons and in swirling lines around the bases.

SMALL CAKES

DID YOU KNOW? The first record of brownies dates back to the year 1896 in the United States.

Hagrid's Hut Rock Cakes

 MAKES 12   10 MINS   15 MINS

Less rocky and more crumbly than Hagrid's version (which have been known to cost the eater a few teeth), these fruity rock cakes are guaranteed to turn any frown upside down, especially if you picture yourself in Hagrid's hut while eating them, next to a roaring fire and a snoozing Fang. Best served with a nice cup of tea or a cold glass of milk.

V

- 1¾ cups/220 g all-purpose flour
- 2 tsp baking powder
- 1 tsp pumpkin pie spice
- 1 stick/110 g unsalted butter, firm, diced
- Zest of 1 lemon, finely grated
- Good pinch of salt
- ¾ cup/135 g dried mixed fruit
- ½ cup/100 g granulated white sugar
- 1 large egg
- 2 tbsp dairy milk
- 6-8 white sugar cubes

1. Preheat the oven to 400°F/200°C/gas mark 6. Line a large baking sheet with baking parchment. Put the flour, baking powder, and pumpkin pie spice in a bowl and rub the butter into the flour with your fingertips until the mixture resembles fine bread crumbs.

2. Stir in the lemon zest, salt, dried mixed fruit, and sugar. Beat the egg with the milk in a small bowl and add to the dry ingredients. Stir well, until the ingredients bind together in a firm dough.

3. Place 12 even-sized spoonfuls of the dough on the baking sheet. There's no need to make neat shapes; they can be craggy! Put the sugar cubes in a small bag and tap with a rolling pin to break up slightly. Scatter over the cakes and bake for 15 minutes, until risen and pale golden. Transfer to a wire rack to cool.

MAGICAL FACT

Two versions of Hagrid's hut were built for the movie series. There was a giant one to make Harry, Ron, and Hermione look smaller and a regular-sized one to make Hagrid look bigger.

> "Mad and hairy? You wouldn't be talking about me, now, would you?"
>
> —RUBEUS HAGRID
> *Harry Potter and the Chamber of Secrets*

SMALL CAKES

TOP TIP

These are best eaten warm or on the day they're baked— but that's okay as they're so easy to make!

Sorting Hat Cupcakes

MAKES 8 • **1–1½ HOURS** • **40 MINS**

Are you brave and true like a Gryffindor? Or resourceful and ambitious like a Slytherin? Perhaps you're witty and intelligent like a Ravenclaw? Or loyal and hard-working like a Hufflepuff? These delectable Sorting Hat cupcakes will help you decide once and for all which Hogwarts house you belong in. And if you can't make your mind up, you'll just have to have another one!

V

FOR THE COOKIES

¾ cup/95 g all-purpose flour

Good pinch of salt

1 stick/110 g unsalted butter, firm, diced

3 tbsp cocoa powder

⅓ cup/40 g confectioners'/icing sugar

1 egg yolk

FOR THE SPONGE

¾ stick/85 g butter, softened

⅓ cup/70 g granulated white sugar

⅔ cup/85 g all-purpose flour

¾ tsp baking powder

1 large egg

1 large egg yolk

Few drops of natural red, blue, green, and yellow food colorings

TO DECORATE

⅔ cup/100 g plain chocolate chips

½ stick/55 g unsalted butter, softened

1 cup/225 g cream cheese

¾ cup/95 g confectioners'/icing sugar

2 tbsp cocoa powder

3 tbsp chocolate or caramel spread

SPECIAL EQUIPMENT

3 inch/7.5 cm cookie cutter

1½ inch/4 cm cookie cutter

¼ inch/0.5 cm piping tube

Large piping bag

6½ x 3 inch/16.5 x 7.5 cm loaf tin

Palette knife

1. Preheat the oven to 350°F/180°C/gas mark 4. Line a baking sheet with baking parchment. Put the flour and salt into a bowl, add the butter and rub in with your fingertips. Stir in the cocoa powder, sugar, and egg yolk and mix to a firm dough. Turn out onto a lightly floured board and shape into a thick log, about 4½ inches/11.5 cms long.

2. Cut into eight even-sized slices. Place a 3 inch/7.5 cm cookie cutter on the baking sheet. Take a slice of the dough and flatten it out inside the cutter. Lift away the cutter and shape seven more cookies in the same way. Bake for 15 minutes and leave to cool on the paper.

3. For the sponge, grease and line a 6½ x 3 inch/16.5 x 7.5 cm loaf tin with baking parchment. Put the butter, sugar, flour, baking powder, egg, and egg yolk in a bowl and beat until smooth and creamy.

4. Divide the mixture into four and spoon three-quarters into different bowls or mugs. Beat a different food coloring into each of the mixtures. Spoon the four different colors, evenly spaced in a line, into the tin. Spread level and bake for about 25 minutes, until just firm to the touch. Transfer to a wire rack to cool.

5. To make the frosting, melt the chocolate chips and leave to cool. In a separate bowl, beat the butter until smooth. Beat in the cream cheese, then the sugar, cocoa powder, and cooled chocolate. Place in a large piping bag fitted with a ¼ inch/0.5 cm piping tube.

6. From each of the sponge colors, cut out two deep rounds using a 1½ inch/4 cm cutter. Trim off the top edges of each to make the shapes slightly conical. Secure one to each of the cookie bases with a dot of chocolate or caramel spread.

7. Take the bag of frosting and pipe around and over the sponges, working to a tip at the top of each. Use the back of a teaspoon or small palette knife to smooth out the frosting. Use the handle end of the teaspoon to indent a mouth and eyes in each.

SMALL CAKES

TOP TIP Play around with shaping the features on the hats. If you're not happy with the faces, simply smooth the frosting over and have another go!

HOUSE-ELF CARROT CUPCAKES

 MAKES 9   **1½–2 HOURS, PLUS COOLING**   **20–25 MINS**

Dobby the house-elf's magical meddling may sometimes backfire (like the time Harry and Ron are unable to access platform nine and three-quarters and end up flying Ron's dad's invisible car to Hogwarts), but his intentions are always good. These mouthwatering carrot cupcakes celebrate Dobby and his fellow house-elves and wouldn't be out of place at a Hogwarts feast.

FOR THE CUPCAKES
- 1½ cups/220 g gluten-free all-purpose flour
- 1 tsp gluten-free baking powder
- ½ tsp xanthan gum
- 1 tsp pumpkin pie spice
- ¾ cup/170 g light brown sugar
- 2 medium carrots, finely grated
- ⅓ cup/60 g sultanas or raisins
- ⅔ cup/150 ml vegetable oil
- 2 large eggs, beaten

TO DECORATE
- 1 stick/110 g unsalted butter, softened
- 1¼ cups/155 g confectioners'/icing sugar
- Natural green food coloring
- 12 oz/350 g beige-colored fondant
- Small piece white fondant
- Small piece brown fondant
- Tube of brown or chocolate-flavor decorator frosting

SPECIAL EQUIPMENT
- Muffin tray
- 9 paper liners
- Palette knife

1. Preheat the oven to 350°F/180°C/gas mark 4. Line a muffin tray with nine paper liners. For the cupcakes, combine the flour, baking powder, xanthan gum, pumpkin pie spice, sugar, carrots, and sultanas or raisins in a bowl. Mix together the oil and eggs and add to the bowl. Stir until evenly mixed, and divide among the cases.

2. Bake for 20-25 minutes, until firm to the touch. Transfer to a wire rack and leave to cool.

3. To decorate, put the butter and sugar in a bowl and beat until smooth and creamy. Stir in a little green food coloring. Spoon a little onto each cupcake and spread right to the edges with a palette knife.

4. For each elf's face, take a small piece of beige-colored fondant, about the size of a walnut, and flatten out to a squat pear shape. Impress a thin mouth shape at the pointed end and place on a cupcake. Shape and position two very large ears and a large pointed nose. Roll small oval shapes in white fondant and position for eyes, adding thin strips of beige-colored fondant for upper and lower lids. Shape and position the top of the body, adding the clothing in brown fondant.

5. Mark wrinkles on the face with the tip of a sharp knife. Paint the centers of the eyes with green food coloring. Finish with dots of brown or chocolate decorator fondant for the middle of the eyes and the hair.

TOP TIP
These carrot cupcakes are very quick and easy to bake, but decorating them takes a lot of molding and shaping. Have fun and play around with it!

SMALL CAKES

DID YOU KNOW?
Although the origins for carrot cake are disputed, the countries of England, France, and Switzerland are commonly lauded as the "inventors" of the dish.

MAGICAL FACT
In the wizarding world, a house-elf is freed when their master or mistress presents them with clothing, such as a sock.

"You shall not harm Harry Potter!"
—DOBBY
Harry Potter and the Chamber of Secrets

SMALL CAKES
87

Hermione's Beaded Bag Cake

SERVES 12-14 · 2 HOURS, PLUS COOLING · 50 MINS

Despite its small size, Hermione's beaded bag is capable of holding clothes, books, medical supplies, and even a tent, thanks to an Undetectable Extension Charm the clever witch places upon it. This sumptuous red velvet cake replica is also full of hidden surprises, as you'll discover when you take your first bite (quickly followed by a second and a third, we're sure).

FOR THE RED VELVET CAKE

2 cups/250 g all-purpose flour

2 tsp baking powder

1 tbsp cocoa powder

2/3 cup/135 g granulated white sugar

2 small raw beets, coarsely grated

6 tbsp vegetable oil

2 large eggs

1 large egg yolk

¾ cup/175 ml buttermilk

1 tbsp white wine vinegar

TO DECORATE

½ stick/55 g unsalted butter, softened

2/3 cup/150 g cream cheese

1¾ cup/220 g confectioners'/icing sugar

Natural purple food coloring

3½ oz/100 g piece purple fondant

Handful of chewy red fruit candies

3 red fruit jelly candies

SPECIAL EQUIPMENT

Two 4 cup/1 liter ovenproof pudding bowls

2 paper or plastic piping bags

¼ inch/0.5 cm plain piping tube

Palette knife

1. Preheat the oven to 325°F/160°C/gas mark 3. Grease two 4 cup/1 liter ovenproof pudding bowls and line the bases with circles of baking parchment. Combine the flour, baking powder, cocoa powder, and sugar in a bowl. Blend the beets, oil, eggs, and egg yolk in a food processor or blender to make a puree. Add to the dry ingredients with the buttermilk and vinegar and mix to a smooth batter.

2. Divide between the bowls and spread level. Bake for about 50 minutes, until risen and firm to the touch. A fine skewer inserted into the center of the cakes should come out clean. Leave to cool in the bowls.

3. To decorate, beat the butter in a bowl until smooth. Beat in the cream cheese. Add the confectioners' sugar and beat until evenly combined. Transfer 3 tablespoons to a separate bowl and stir purple food coloring into the remainder. If the frosting seems loose and too soft to spread, chill in the fridge for an hour or so to firm up.

4. Cut the domed surface off the two cakes and sandwich the cakes together with a little purple frosting. Place on a serving plate. Using a palette knife, spread a thin layer of purple frosting all over the cake.

5. Put the remainder in a piping bag fitted with a ¼ inch/0.5 cm plain piping tube. Pipe a wavy line of frosting around the top of the cake. Pipe another two lines of frosting over this to build up the depth. Chill while shaping the decorations.

6. Take a little of the purple fondant and roll as thin as you can under the palms of your hands. Roll a second piece in the same way and then twist the two pieces together to resemble rope. Arrange this roped decoration over the piped frosting.

BIG CAKES

7. Roll and cut out five rectangles of fondant, each measuring 3 x 1 inch/7.5 x 2.5 cm. Press gently around the sides of the cake. Halve the chewy candies and arrange in vertical rows between the fondant panels. Shape and arrange two further ropes of fondant, each about 8 inches/20 cms long, and let these trail from the cake.

8. Thinly roll out a 2½ x 1 inch/6 x 2.5 cm rectangle of fondant and make deep lengthwise cuts, keeping the fondant intact at one short end. Roll up and position at the base of the cake for the tassel. Position the three jelly candies as shown. Put the reserved frosting in a piping bag and snip off the tip so the frosting can be piped in a thin line. Use to pipe decorations over the fondant panels and the jelly candies.

MAGICAL FACT

Hermione's beaded bag is David Yates's favorite prop from the films. Yates directed the last four Harry Potter movies, from the Order of the Phoenix to the Deathly Hallows — Part 2.

TOP TIP

Make the presentation even more special by arranging Harry Potter chess figures or chocolate chess pieces on the squares.

WIZARD'S CHESS SQUARES

 SERVES 16   40 MINS, PLUS COOLING   40 MINS

"Knight to H3!" This brainy bake lets you create your own version of wizard's chess, which, as everyone knows, is much cooler than ordinary chess. (The pieces move themselves, for starters!) Will you play it safe like Percy Weasley or risk it all like Ron? Whatever tactics you choose, everyone's a winner, as it all tastes so heavenly!

V GF

1. Preheat the oven to 375°F/190°C/gas mark 5. Line the base and sides of a 7 inch/18 cm square cake tin with baking parchment. To make the light squares, put the butter, honey, sugar, and orange zest in a saucepan and heat gently until the butter has melted.

2. Remove from the heat and stir in the oats. Transfer to the tin, level the surface, and bake for 20 minutes, or until pale golden. Leave in the tin for 10 minutes, then transfer to a wire rack to cool.

3. To make the dark squares, reline the tin with baking parchment. Melt the butter with the maple syrup and sugar. Stir in the oats and cocoa powder and level the surface. Bake for 20 minutes, then cool as above.

4. To assemble, carefully cut each of the squares into 6 even-sized bars, then cut across in the opposite direction so you have 36 squares of each. Choose a flat, square serving platter or board and assemble the squares in a checkerboard design of 8 squares wide. (You'll have a few spares in each flavor just in case.) Cover and keep in a cool place until ready to serve.

FOR THE LIGHT SQUARES

1½ sticks/165 g unsalted butter, diced

⅓ cup/75 ml honey

½ cup/100 g granulated white sugar

Zest of 1 large orange, finely grated

2¾ cups/275 g gluten-free porridge oats

FOR THE DARK SQUARES

1½ sticks/165 g unsalted butter, diced

¼ cup/75 ml maple syrup

½ cup/100 g granulated white sugar

2½ cups/250 g gluten-free porridge oats

⅓ cup/45 g cocoa powder

SPECIAL EQUIPMENT

7 inch/18 cm square cake tin

VG — For a vegan version, use dairy-free butter and maple syrup rather than honey in the light squares.

TOP TIP
The squares are easier to cut neatly into squares if you make them several hours in advance or even the day before serving.

INDIVIDUAL BAKES

Hogwarts House Meringues

MAKES 12 — **40 MINS, PLUS COOLING AND CHILLING** — **1 HOUR**

With a variety of tasty fruit fillings—blueberries for Ravenclaw, raspberries for Gryffindor, kiwi fruit for Slytherin, and bananas for Hufflepuff—these colorful and yummy meringues are a wonderful way to demonstrate your house pride!

V **GF**

FOR THE MERINGUES

4 large egg whites
1 cup/200 g granulated white sugar

TO FINISH

Natural red, green, yellow and blue liquid or gel food colorings (see Fillings)

1. Preheat the oven to 275°F/140°C/gas mark 1. Line two baking sheets with baking parchment.

2. Whisk the egg whites in a thoroughly clean bowl until just peaking. Add a tablespoon of the sugar and whisk again for about 15 seconds. Add another spoonful of the sugar. Continue to whisk the mixture, gradually adding the remaining sugar in the same way, until the meringue is thick and glossy.

3. Place tablespoons of the meringue onto the baking sheets, spacing them slightly apart. You should have enough mixture for 12 little mounds.

4. To ripple the meringues with color, add a drop or two of your chosen food coloring to a meringue and swirl in with a teaspoon. Repeat with the remainder. Bake for about 1 hour, until crisp on the surface. Leave to cool on the baking sheet.

5. Sandwich the meringues together in pairs using the chosen fillings and keep in a cool place until ready to serve.

FILLINGS

Choose your favorite house and make the meringues in a single color and flavor or, mix them up and make a few of all four.

RAVENCLAW

Heat 2/3 cup/100 g mashed blueberries in a small saucepan with 2 teaspoons granulated white sugar and 1 teaspoon lemon juice until the berries have softened. Leave to cool, then add ½ cup/120 ml heavy cream and whisk until the mixture holds its shape, adding a dash of blue food coloring. Chill until needed.

GRYFFINDOR

Mash ½ cup/75 g raspberries in a bowl. Add ½ cup/120 ml heavy cream and whisk until the mixture holds its shape, adding a dash of red food coloring. Chill until needed.

SLYTHERIN

Mash or blend 1 large kiwi fruit. Add ½ cup/120 ml heavy cream and whisk until the mixture holds its shape, adding a dash of green food coloring. Chill until needed.

HUFFLEPUFF

Mash 1 banana in a bowl with 2 teaspoons of lemon or lime juice. Add ½ cup/120 ml heavy cream and whisk until the mixture holds its shape, adding a dash of yellow food coloring. Chill until needed.

INDIVIDUAL BAKES

DID YOU KNOW? Meringues are commonly believed to be of Swiss origin, with lots of influence from French and Italian chefs. The first record of the word "meringue" dates back to the year 1692.

MANDRAKE BREAD

SERVES 8 | **1½ HOURS, PLUS PROOFING** | **30 MINS**

You don't need protective earmuffs to make our version of this screeching magical plant from *Harry Potter and the Chamber of Secrets*, but that doesn't mean you won't be "knocked out" by the finished dish. Moist and filling with a cherry, chocolate, and nut center, it's the perfect sweet treat for any time of day.

1. Put the flours and salt in a bowl and rub in the butter with your fingertips. Stir in the yeast, sugar, egg, vanilla, and milk and mix to form a dough, adding a dash more milk if the dough is dry and crumbly.

2. Turn out onto a floured surface and knead for 10 minutes, until smooth and elastic. Place in a lightly oiled bowl, cover with plastic wrap, and leave in a warm place for about two hours, until the dough has doubled in size.

3. Line a large baking sheet with baking parchment. Combine the candied cherries, milk chocolate chips, and chopped mixed nuts in a bowl.

4. Punch the dough to deflate it, and turn out onto a floured surface. Cut off and reserve a sixth of the dough. Cut the remainder into three even-sized pieces and roll out each to a long thin strip measuring 18 x 4 inches/46 x 10 cms. Sprinkle the cherry mixture along the center of each strip. Bring the edges of the strips up over the filling and pinch firmly together to seal in the filling and create long, thin sausage-like shapes.

5. Turn the pieces over so the seams are underneath. Pinch the three pieces firmly together at one end and then braid together. Scrunch up the shaped dough, making it thinner at the ends and slightly wider in the center. Transfer to the baking sheet and measure the length. It should be about 12 inches/30 cms.

6. Quarter the reserved piece of dough. Roll two pieces under the palms of your hands until about 10 inches/25 cms long. Make deep cuts into one end of each with a sharp knife to resemble roots. Tuck under the sides of the braid for arms. Do the same with the remaining pieces of dough, rolling them to about 5 inches/12.5 cms long and tucking under the lower end of the braid.

Continues overleaf.

FOR THE DOUGH

2¼ cups/280 g whole wheat bread flour

2 cups/250 g white bread flour

1 tsp salt

½ stick/55 g unsalted butter, firm, diced

1½ tsp active dry yeast

¼ cup/50 g granulated white sugar

1 large egg, beaten

1 tbsp vanilla extract

1 cup/250 ml warm dairy milk

TO FINISH

½ cup/75 g chopped candied cherries

½ cup/75 g milk chocolate chips

½ cup/60 g chopped mixed nuts

¼ cup/40 g chocolate chips

Several sprigs of bay leaves

SPECIAL EQUIPMENT

Small paper or plastic piping bag

> "The Mandrake's cry is fatal to anyone who hears it."
> —HERMIONE GRANGER
> *Harry Potter and the Chamber of Secrets*

MAGICAL FACTS

Although the cry of an adult Mandrake will kill you, the cry of a Mandrake Seedling (like the one in our bake) will only knock you out for several hours. Phew, that's all right, then!

In the wizarding world, the Mandrake or mandragora plant is used to return those who've been petrified to their original state. Which is quite handy when there's a Basilisk on the loose!

BREADS

7   Cover loosely with oiled plastic wrap and leave in a warm place for 30 minutes. Preheat the oven to 400°F/200°C/gas mark 6.

8   Press the handle end of a spoon or fork into the bread at the head end to shape two eyes and a mouth. Bake for about 30 minutes, until risen and deep golden, covering loosely with foil if the bread gets too brown. Leave to cool on the baking sheet.

9   Melt the chocolate and spoon into a small piping bag. Snip off the tip and pipe the chocolate into the eye and mouth cavities. Pipe the remainder over the root ends of the limbs. Push the sprigs of bay leaves into the head end of the bread to finish.

DID YOU KNOW?
When designing Greenhouse Three, where Harry and his fellow second-years have their Herbology lessons, the film's design team drew inspiration from the Royal Botanic Gardens in Kew, London.

TOP TIP
If you want to get ahead, freeze this bread before adding the chocolate decorations and leaves. Warm it through in a moderate oven after thawing, then finish the decorations. It's also delicious served buttered!

MAGICAL FACT
Although the screaming Mandrakes in the Harry Potter films are fictional, the Mandrake plant is very real. It is often found in the Mediterranean.

Hogwarts Treacle Tart

 SERVES 8   45 MINS, PLUS PROOFING   1 HOUR

A firm favorite of Harry's, this juicy treacle tart will have you reaching for your dessert spoon the moment it leaves the oven (although make sure you give it a few minutes to cool before you tuck in). Top with your Hogwarts house animal of choice for added wizarding cred!

FOR THE PASTRY
- 1¾ cups/220 g all-purpose flour
- 1⅓ stick/150 g unsalted butter, firm, diced
- 1 large egg yolk
- 2 tbsp granulated white sugar

FOR THE FILLING
- 2¾ cups/550 g granulated white sugar
- ½ stick/55 g unsalted butter, diced
- Zest, finely grated, and juice of 3 lemons
- 1½ cups/115 g fresh white bread crumbs
- 3 large eggs, beaten

TO DECORATE
- 2 tbsp confectioners'/icing sugar

SPECIAL EQUIPMENT
- 9 inch/23 cm round loose-base tart tin with a 1¼ inch/4 cm depth
- Pie weights/baking beans

1. To make the pastry, put the flour in a bowl and rub in the butter with your fingertips until the mixture resembles coarse bread crumbs. Add the egg yolk, sugar, and 2 tablespoons of cold water and mix to form a firm dough. Wrap with plastic wrap and chill for 30 minutes.

2. Preheat the oven to 400°F/200°C/gas mark 6. Roll out the pastry on a lightly floured surface and use to line a 9 inch/23 cm tart tin with a 1¼ inch/4 cm depth. Line with baking parchment and fill with pie weights/baking beans.

3. Bake for 20 minutes. Remove the paper and pie weights/baking beans and reduce the oven temperature to 350°F/180°C/gas mark 4.

4. To make the filling, put the sugar in a heavy-based saucepan with ½ cup/120 ml water and heat very gently, until the sugar has dissolved. Increase the heat and let the syrup bubble for about 10 minutes, until it has turned to a deep amber color. Dip the base of the pan in cold water to prevent further cooking.

TOP TIP

Making sugar syrup, as in step 3, takes time and patience! Make sure you use a good quality, heavy-based saucepan and thoroughly dissolve the sugar before increasing the heat. Keep a close watch on it after that, as the syrup will quickly turn dark and bitter, and eventually burn.

This syrup is a homemade version of "golden syrup," which is a traditional ingredient of Harry's favorite tart. If you can get hold of it, use 1½ cups/475 g golden syrup instead, and skip making your own.

← This tart has a lovely lemon flavor.

PASTRY

5 Add the butter, lemon juice, and zest to the pan and stir until completely smooth. If the syrup gets hard and doesn't dissolve into the liquid, stir over a gentle heat until it does. Stir in the bread crumbs and eggs and turn the filling into the tin. Bake for 30-40 minutes, until the filling is lightly set.

6 While baking, trace and cut out the Hogwarts Treacle Tart template on page 115. Once the tart has finished baking, rest the template over the center of the tart. Put the confectioners' sugar in a tea strainer or small sieve and sprinkle over the template so the surface is coated in a fine dusting of sugar. Carefully lift away the template. This is easiest done by gently sliding a palette knife under the template and quickly lifting it up.

TOP TIP

We've topped our tart with the Hufflepuff badger (see page 115 for the template), but you could just as easily draw and use the Gryffindor lion, Ravenclaw raven, or Slytherin snake.

DID YOU KNOW?

Treacle tarts can be served hot as well as cold.

Fluttery Flying Key Cookies

 MAKES 16-18　　 45 MINS　　 10 MINS

In the first film, Harry, Ron, and Hermione must navigate a series of dangerous obstacles including Filius Flitwick's winged keys, which the professor has enchanted using a flying charm. Conjure up your own—hopefully less elusive—flock of keys with this fun and simple recipe. The nutty taste of these cookies will definitely leave you all aflutter!

FOR THE COOKIES

1 large egg white

¼ cup/50 g golden granulated white sugar

½ cup/55 g ground hazelnuts

TO DECORATE

Several sheets of rice paper

Tube of gold decorator frosting

SPECIAL EQUIPMENT

Paper or plastic piping bag

¼ inch/0.5 cm plain piping tube

1. Preheat the oven to 350°F/180°C/gas mark 4. Trace and cut out the two Fluttery Flying Keys templates on page 116. Line a large baking sheet with baking parchment.

2. Whisk the egg white in a thoroughly clean bowl until peaking. Gradually whisk in the sugar, a spoonful at a time, until thick and glossy. Stir in the ground hazelnuts. Place the mixture in a piping bag fitted with a ¼ inch/0.5 cm plain piping tube.

3. Slide the key template under the paper on the baking sheet and pipe over, starting with a loop at the top end and finishing in a straight line to the end. Pipe a ½ inch/1 cm line next to this for the bit. Reposition the template and pipe more keys in the same way.

4. Bake for about 10 minutes, until pale golden and lightly crisped. Leave to cool before carefully lifting away from the paper.

5. Cut around the wings template onto rice paper. You should be able to cut out several thicknesses of paper at the same time. Pipe lines onto the cookies with decorator frosting, as shown. Secure the wings in place with dots of frosting from the tube and bend some of the wings upright if you like.

MAGICAL FACT

Actor Warwick Davis, who plays Filius Flitwick, also provides the voice for Griphook the Goblin in the Harry Potter films.

COOKIES

MONSTER BOOK OF MONSTERS

 **SERVES 12-14**   **2½-3 HOURS, PLUS COOLING**   **45-50 MINS**

The Monster Book of Monsters by Edwardus Lima is as much a sentient being as the fantastic beasts within its pages—and a bad-tempered one at that. This amazing banana-fused version won't try to bite off your fingers, but we do recommend stroking the spine before you cut yourself a slice. Just in case!

1. Preheat the oven to 325°F/160°C/gas mark 3. Grease and line an 8 inch/20 cm square cake tin with baking parchment. Beat together the butter, sugar, vanilla, and cinnamon until pale and creamy. Gradually beat in the eggs, a little at a time, adding a spoonful of the flour if the mixture starts to separate. Stir in the mashed bananas. Add the flour and baking powder and stir in until combined.

2. Transfer to the tin and level the surface. Bake for 45-50 minutes, until risen and golden. The surface should be just firm to the touch. Leave in the tin for 5 minutes, then transfer to a wire rack to cool.

3. For the frosting, beat together the sugar and butter until smooth, creamy, and very pale in color. Cut a 1½ inch/4 cm thick slice off one side of the cake and position at one thin end of the cake, trimming off the excess corner to create a rectangle. Lift the cake onto a serving plate or board, securing the two pieces together with a little frosting. Spread a thin layer of frosting over the top and sides of the cake.

4. On a surface dusted with confectioners' sugar, knead a little brown food coloring into the white fondant to color it deep cream. Roll out half the fondant and cut out strips the depth of the cake. Wrap around the sides of the cake, smoothing out the joins.

5. Roll out the other half of the fondant and cut out a rectangle slightly larger than the cake. Lift into position and press down lightly. Use the back of a large knife held horizontally against the cake to press page markings on three sides of the cake.

6. Finish the base edge of three sides with a small strip of fondant, securing in place with a dampened fine paintbrush. Reserve the trimmings.

Continues overleaf.

FOR THE CAKE
1¾ sticks/195 g unsalted butter, softened, plus extra to grease
1 cup/200 g granulated white sugar
2 tsp vanilla extract
1 tsp ground cinnamon
3 large eggs, beaten
3 medium bananas, mashed
1¾ cups/220 g all-purpose flour
2 tsp baking powder

FOR THE FROSTING
2½ cups/315 g confectioners'/icing sugar
1½ sticks/165 g unsalted butter, softened

TO DECORATE
Confectioners'/icing sugar, for kneading
Natural black and brown food coloring
1½ lb/675 g white fondant
2 oz/50 g black fondant
2 oz/50 g brown fondant
Small piece red fondant
Edible gold liquid food coloring

SPECIAL EQUIPMENT
Fine paintbrush
¼ inch/0.5 cm plain piping tube
Large piping bag
8 inch/20 cm square cake tin

BIG CAKES

TOP TIP

Shaping the face and jaw requires a little patience, but it looks so good once you've made it work. Keep molding, and if necessary remolding the fondant until you're happy with it.

Always keep the fondant you're not using tightly wrapped in plastic wrap so it doesn't dry out.

7 Reserve a pea-sized piece of black fondant. Knead the remainder with the brown fondant. Thinly roll out half on a surface dusted with confectioners' sugar and cut out a 3¾ x 3 inch/9.5 x 7.5 cm rectangle and a 3¾ x 1½ inch/9.5 x 4 cm rectangle. Position the larger rectangle at the top of the cake and the smaller one at the bottom, ready for piping the book title on.

8 Knead the trimmings with the remaining fondant and mold into a monster face with slightly pointed snout and wider at the top. Position on the cake between the two rectangles. Shape four pea-sized balls of the reserved cream icing and position for eyes, securing with a dampened paintbrush. Roll tiny balls of the reserved black fondant and secure to the eyes.

9 To make the jaw, mold two semicircular shapes of red fondant. With the white fondant, shape and position pointed teeth. Roll out the red fondant trimmings and cut out a small bookmark ribbon in a slightly curvy tongue shape. Secure the shapes in place. Using a fine paintbrush and gold food coloring, write "The Monster Book of Monsters" onto the fondant rectangles.

BIG CAKES

10 Divide the remaining frosting between two bowls and color one half gray, using black food coloring, and the other brown. Alternate spoonfuls of the frosting in a large piping bag fitted with a ¼ inch/0.5 cm piping tube. Pipe blobs of frosting around the base of the cake and further blobs around the top edges of the cake. If you can, pull the bag away once you've piped a blob so the frosting trails slightly over the edge of the cake.

11 Use the remainder to pipe over the top of the cake and along the "spine." Finish by using a fork to fluff up the frosting to resemble fur.

MAGICAL FACTS

Graphic designer Miraphora Mina made several versions of *The Monster Book of Monsters* for *Harry Potter and the Prisoner of Azkaban*, including one with clawed feet and a spiky tail.

Peek (carefully) inside the movie's version of *The Monster Book of Monsters* and you'll find pages devoted to Hippogriffs, house-elves, and Mandrake Roots, to name but a few.

BIG CAKES

Dumbledore's Sherbet Lemon Rolls

MAKES 14 · **30 MINS, PLUS PROOFING** · **10 MINS**

There are three things everyone knows about Albus Dumbledore. He is proud of his Chocolate Frog card, he's the only wizard Lord Voldemort fears (apart from Harry), and he has a terrible sweet tooth, especially when it comes to sherbet lemons. Celebrate the greatest wizard of his age by whipping up a batch of these tangy, tingly lemon rolls. They're simply the zest!

FOR THE ROLLS
- 3½ cups/440 g white bread flour
- ½ tsp salt
- ½ stick/55 g unsalted butter, chilled, diced
- 1½ tsp active dry yeast
- ⅓ cup/70 g granulated white sugar
- 2 large eggs, beaten
- ⅔ cup/150 ml dairy milk, warmed

TO FINISH
- 14 lemon candies
- 1¾ cups/220 g confectioners'/icing sugar
- Approximately 2 tbsp lemon juice
- Dash of natural yellow food coloring

1. Put the flour and salt in a bowl and rub in the butter with your fingertips. Stir in the yeast, sugar, eggs, and milk and mix to form a dough with a round-bladed knife, adding a dash more milk if the dough is dry and crumbly.

2. Turn out onto a floured surface and knead for 10 minutes, until smooth and elastic. Place in a lightly oiled bowl, cover with plastic wrap, and leave in a warm place for about 1½ hours, until the dough has doubled in size.

3. Line a large baking sheet with baking parchment. Punch the dough to deflate it, and turn out onto a floured surface. Divide the dough into fourteen even-sized pieces.

4. Flatten one piece into an oval shape and push a candy chew lengthwise into the center. Pinch the dough up and over the candy to seal into a finger-shaped roll. Transfer to the baking sheet with the pinched joins underneath. Repeat with the remaining dough and candies.

5. Cover loosely with plastic wrap and leave in a warm place for 30-40 minutes, until risen. Preheat the oven to 400°F/200°C/gas mark 6.

6. Bake the rolls for about 10 minutes, until pale golden. Transfer to a wire rack to cool.

7. Mix together the confectioners' sugar and 1½ tablespoons of the lemon juice. Add a dash of yellow food coloring and more lemon juice, drop by drop, until the frosting is smooth and thickly coats the back of the spoon. It should very slowly become level when left in the bowl. (You might not need all the lemon juice.) Spoon the frosting over the tops of the rolls.

MAGICAL FACT
"Sherbet lemon" is the password to Dumbledore's headmaster's office during Harry's second year at Hogwarts.

TOP TIP
Just a word of caution—don't be tempted to bite into these rolls as soon as they come out of the oven. The filling gets very hot!

SMALL CAKES

TOP TIP
Sprinkle some edible glitter over your rolls to give them a magical sparkle!

PUFFSKEIN CREAM PUFFS

 MAKES 8   1 HOUR, PLUS COOLING   25 MINS

Made of sugar, spice (well, a pinch of salt anyway), and all things nice, these adorable mini pastries are almost too cute to eat. Modeled after the lovable pink and purple creatures sold by Fred and George in Weasleys' Wizard Wheezes, they're so deliciously custardy, as soon as you've polished off one batch, you'll want to make another.

FOR THE PASTRY
- ½ cup/65 g all-purpose flour, plus 1 tbsp
- ½ stick/55 g unsalted butter, diced
- 2 tbsp granulated white sugar
- Good pinch of salt
- 2 large eggs, beaten

FOR THE CUSTARD FILLING
- 1¼ cups/310 ml dairy milk
- 3 large egg yolks
- 3 tbsp granulated white sugar
- 2 tsp vanilla extract
- 3 tbsp cornstarch
- ½ cup/120 ml heavy cream
- ¼ cup/100 g chunky pieces of honeycomb

TO DECORATE
- Tube of white decorator frosting
- 16 cake decorators' candy eyeballs
- 1½ cups/370 ml heavy cream
- 1½ tbsp confectioners'/icing sugar
- Pink food coloring

SPECIAL EQUIPMENT
- ½ inch/1 cm plain piping tube
- ¼ inch/0.5 cm star piping tube
- 2 large paper or plastic piping bags

1. Preheat the oven to 400°F/200°C/gas mark 6. Line a baking sheet with baking parchment. Sift all the flour onto a square of baking parchment.

2. Put the butter, sugar, and salt in a small saucepan with ⅔ cup/150 ml water and heat gently until the butter has melted. Bring to a boil and tip in the flour from the baking parchment. Remove from the heat and beat with a wooden spoon until you have a thick paste. Leave to cool for 5 minutes.

3. Add a little of the egg and beat until absorbed into the paste. Continue beating in the eggs, a little at a time, until the paste is thick and glossy. Put the paste in a large piping bag fitted with a ½ inch/1 cm plain piping tube. Pipe eight large, slightly elongated blobs onto the baking sheet, leaving a generous space between each. Use all the mixture.

4. Bake for 25 minutes, until puffed and golden. Make a small slit on one side of each to let the steam escape and prevent them from turning soggy. Transfer to a wire rack to finish cooling.

5. Meanwhile, make the filling. Put the milk in a small saucepan and heat until simmering. Beat together the egg yolks, sugar, vanilla, and cornstarch in a bowl until smooth. Pour the hot milk into the bowl, whisking well.

6. Return to the heat and cook gently, stirring continuously, until the mixture is very thick. Transfer to a bowl and cover the surface with plastic wrap to prevent a skin forming. Leave to cool.

7. Whip the ½ cup/120 ml cream in a bowl until peaking. Stir into the custard with the honeycomb. Spoon the filling into the buns.

8. Use the white decorator frosting to secure two eyes to one end of each bun. Put the cream, sugar, and a dash of pink food coloring into a bowl and beat until just holding its shape. Spoon into a piping bag fitted with a ¼ inch/0.5 cm star piping tube and pipe blobs over the tops of the buns. Chill until ready to serve.

According to Luna Lovegood, Puffskeins have been known to sing on Boxing Day.

SMALL CAKES

MAGICAL FACT

Puffskeins are small magical beasts with fluffy fur. Ginny Weasley purchases one as a pet from her brothers' joke shop in *Harry Potter and the Half-Blood Prince*. Rather brilliantly, she names him Arnold!

DID YOU KNOW? Cream puffs, also known as profiteroles and choux puffs, are often served at French and Italian celebrations.

Knitted Sweater Cookies

MAKES 12 | **1 HOUR, PLUS CHILLING** | **15 MINS**

Molly Weasley's knitted sweaters are crafted with love, and Harry is touched to receive one in the first film—it's one of his first proper presents! Make your own versions of these brilliant Christmas sweaters with this easy-to-follow bake. With twelve in a batch, you could even personalize them for all of your family and friends.

V | **GF**

FOR THE COOKIES

- 1⅓ sticks/150 g unsalted butter, softened
- ⅔ cup/85 g confectioners'/icing sugar
- Good pinch of salt
- 2 tsp ground ginger
- 2 large egg yolks
- 1½ cups/220 g gluten-free all-purpose flour
- 1½ tsp xanthan gum

TO DECORATE

- ¾ stick/85 g unsalted butter, softened
- 1¾ cups/220 g confectioners'/icing sugar
- Natural green and red food coloring
- Tube of gold or yellow decorator frosting

SPECIAL EQUIPMENT

2 small paper or plastic piping bags
"Basket weave" piping tube

1. Beat together the butter, sugar, salt, and ginger until pale and creamy. Gradually beat in the egg yolks. Stir in the flour and xanthan gum to make a smooth, firm dough. Wrap and chill for 2 hours.

2. Line a large baking sheet with baking parchment. Trace and cut out the Knitted Sweater Cookies template on page 116. Thinly roll out the dough on a lightly floured surface and cut around the template with a small sharp knife. Transfer the shapes to the baking sheet and chill for 30 minutes. Preheat the oven to 350°C/180°C/gas mark 4.

3. Bake the cookies for 15 minutes, or until pale golden around the edges. Leave to cool on the baking sheet.

4. To decorate, put the butter and sugar in a bowl and beat until pale and creamy. Transfer half to a separate bowl. Color one bowl with green food coloring and one bowl with red. Put the green frosting in a piping bag fitted with a basket weave tube. Pipe the frosting over half the cookies, starting with the sleeves and finishing with the collar.

5. Wash the tube, fit into a clean piping bag, and fill with the red frosting. Pipe the remaining cookies in the same way.

6. Use the gold or yellow decorator frosting to pipe a "H" on the green cookies and an "R" on the red ones. Keep in a cool place until ready to eat.

TOP TIP

These cute cookies can be baked a day ahead and stored in an airtight container so they don't soften. Decorate them on the day of serving.

DID YOU KNOW? Cheesecake has ancient origins—ancient Greece, that is! The first recorded mention of cheesecake was by the Greek physician Aegimus in the fifth century BCE.

The Burrow Chocolate Cheesecake

SERVES 10-12 | **1-1½ HOURS, PLUS COOLING** | **ABOUT 1 HOUR**

Ramshackle and chaotic—seven kids will do that!—but also warm and filled with color, the Weasleys' family home, The Burrow, is a place where Harry always feels welcome. This scrumptious bake shows you how to build a cheesecake replica of Molly and Arthur's amazing wizarding house, only instead of magic, we've used chocolate finger cookies to hold it all together. Yum!

1. Preheat the oven to 325°F/160°C/gas mark 3. Line the base and sides of an 8 inch/20 cm square cake tin with baking parchment. For the cheesecake base, melt the butter in a saucepan.

2. Reserve one of the sandwich cookies. Put the remainder in a bag and crush with a rolling pin to make fine crumbs. Add to the pan and mix well. Reserve 3 tablespoons of the mixture and pack the remainder into the tin. Pack down firmly and chill while making the filling.

3. Melt the chocolate. Beat the cream cheese in a bowl until smooth, then gradually beat in the eggs and cream. Stir in the chocolate and spoon over the cookie base, spreading in an even layer.

4. Bake for about 1 hour, or until the cheesecake feels only just firm. (It'll firm up further as it cools.) Leave to cool, preferably overnight (see Top Tip).

5. Place the cheesecake on a board and peel away the sides of the paper lining. Using diagram 1, overleaf, cut out the sections of The Burrow and assemble the pieces on a large board or tray, as in diagram 2. To keep the knife cuts clean, wipe the knife after each cut. Some of the shapes are turned upside down to represent different parts of the house.

Continues overleaf.

FOR THE CHEESECAKE
- ¾ stick/85 g unsalted butter, diced
- Two 5½ oz/150 g packs chocolate sandwich cookies
- 3 cups/450 g white chocolate chips
- 2¼ cups/510 g cream cheese
- 3 large eggs
- ⅔ cup/150 ml heavy cream

TO DECORATE
- Plenty of chocolate finger cookies
- Tube of milk chocolate decorator frosting

SPECIAL EQUIPMENT
8 inch/20 cm square cake tin

TOP TIP
The cheesecake is best made a day ahead so it has plenty of time to firm up overnight. This will make slicing it much easier.

BIG CAKES

6. Arrange the chocolate finger cookies over the cheesecake as shown in the photograph. Use the chocolate decorator frosting to pipe the doors and windows onto the cheesecake.

7. Halve the reserved cookie and position at the top of the front door and upper window. Take a small piece of the reserved crumb base and position for the door knob. Scatter the remaining crumbs along the base of the house. Keep in a cool place until ready to serve.

TOP TIP If you can't get ahold of chocolate decorator frosting, melt a little milk chocolate and put in a paper piping bag. Snip off the tip so you can pipe the chocolate in a fine line.

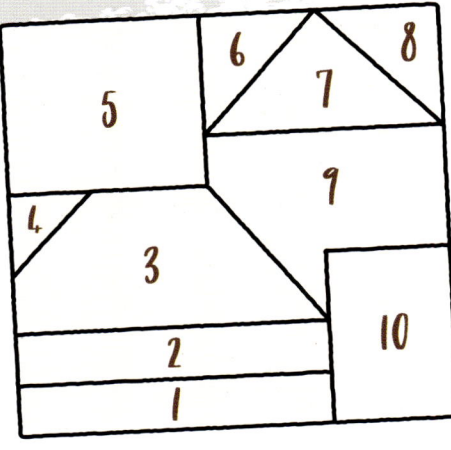

Use this diagram (1) to cut your cheesecake into the shapes you'll need for The Burrow.

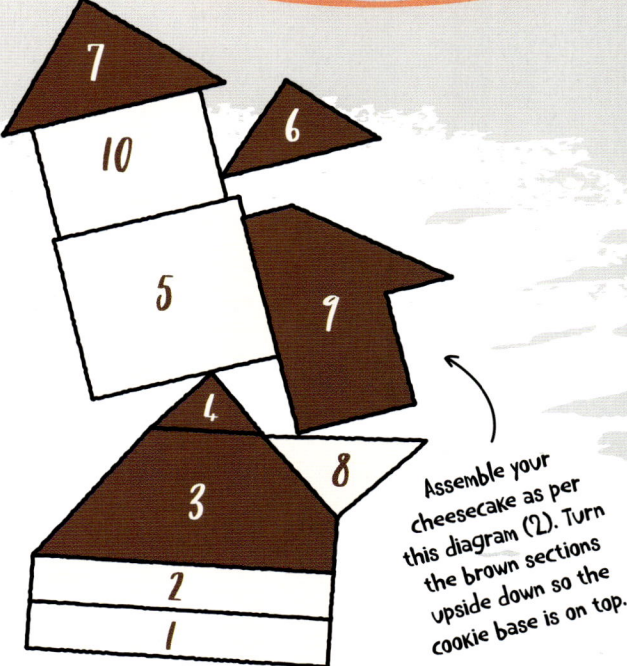

Assemble your cheesecake as per this diagram (2). Turn the brown sections upside down so the cookie base is on top.

MAGICAL FACT

In *Harry Potter and the Half-Blood Prince*, The Burrow is burned down by Death Eaters. Rather than destroy the established set, which they knew they'd need again, the production team built a replica Burrow, about a third of the size. "It took six months to build and six minutes to burn down," remembers assistant art director Gary Tomkins.

BIG CAKES

Templates

Trace and cut out these templates to use with your bakes.

Gryffindor Sword Cookies

Hogwarts Treacle Tart

cut out and discard dotted line sections

Great Lake Merperson Tart

TEMPLATES

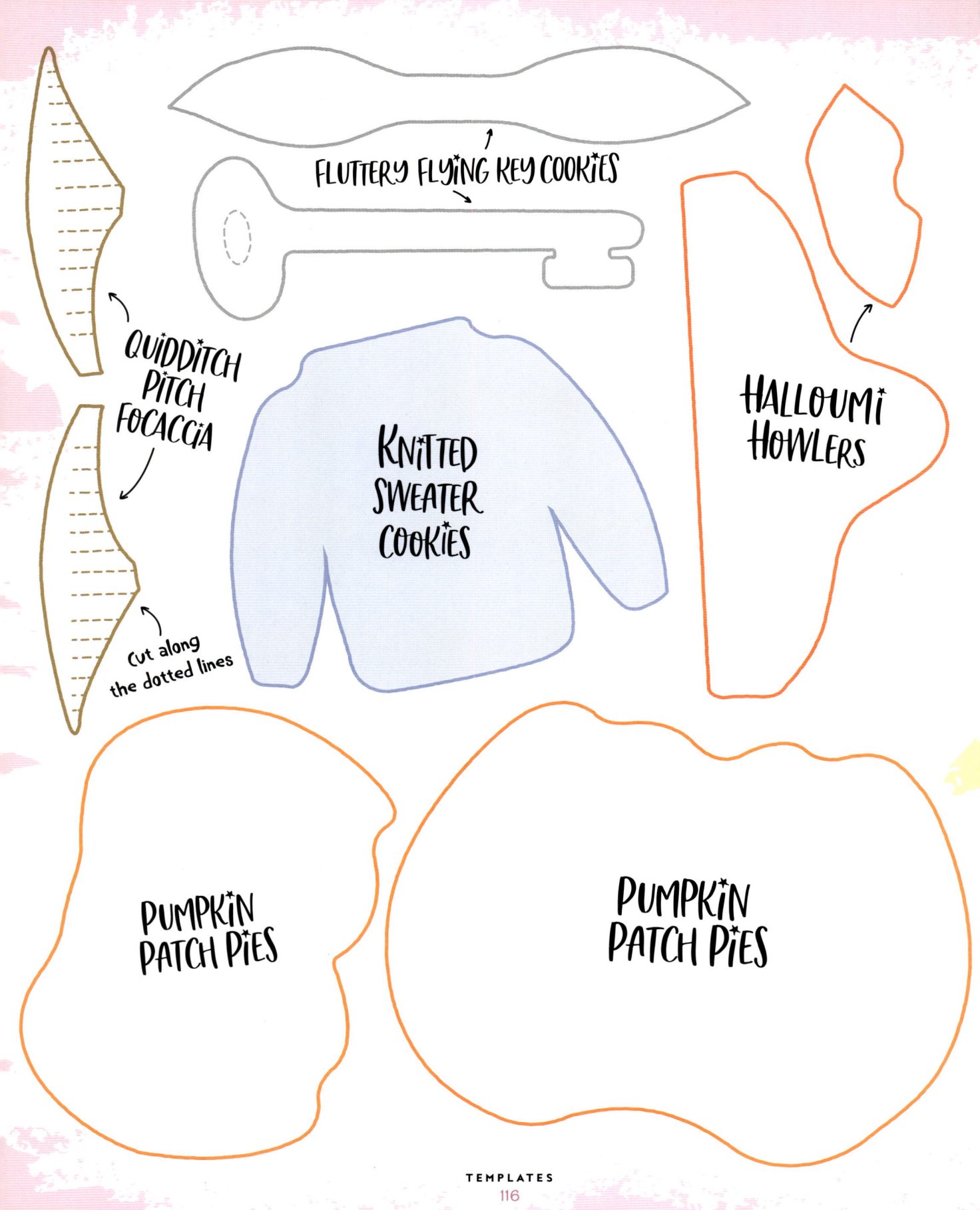

Hogwarts Crest Pie

TEMPLATES
118

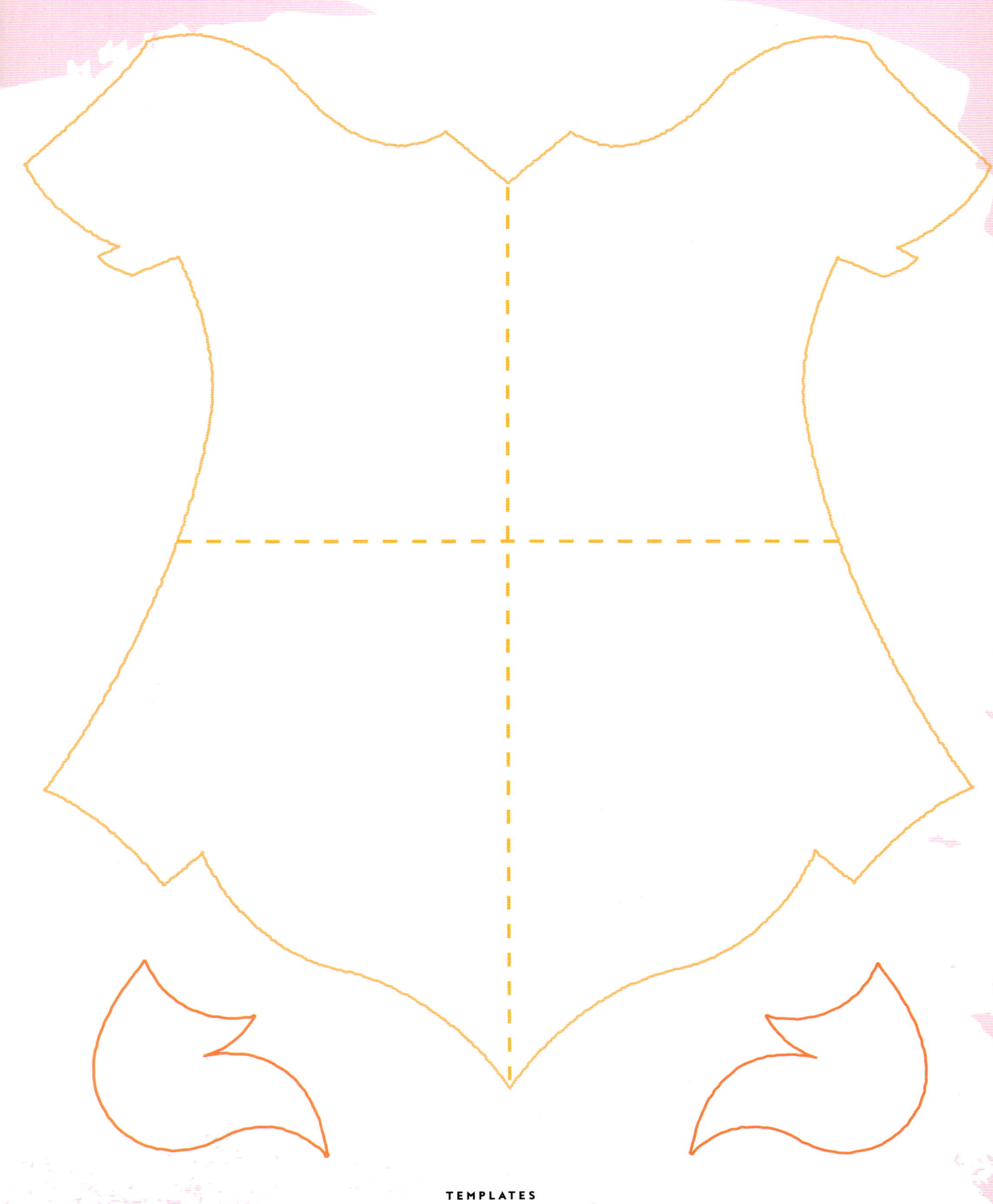

TEMPLATES
119

HOGWARTS GINGERBREAD CASTLE

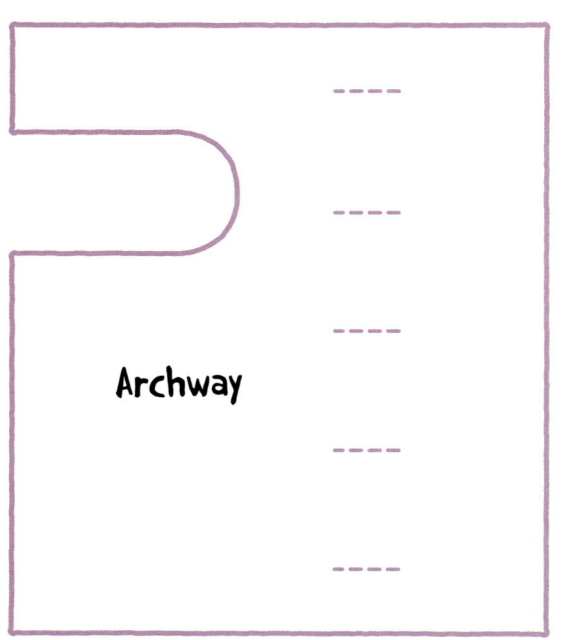

Archway

Great Hall Roof

School of Witchcraft and Wizardry Roof
x 2

Tower
x 4

Great Hall Sides
x 2

TEMPLATES

Tower Top

Great Hall Ends
x 2

Cut the door on one end

School of Witchcraft and Wizardry Ends
x 2

School of Witchcraft and Wizardry Roof Sides
x 2

Use these dotted lines to mark the windows. These should be pressed into your gingerbread using a flat utensil handle.

INDEX

A

almond milk
Wand Breadsticks 14

almonds
Dragon-Roasted-Nut Tarts 60
Gryffindor Sword Cookies 66
Salazar Slytherin's Sourdough Snake 18
Savory Owl Muffins 30

B

bacon
Great Lake Tart 28
Pumpkin Patch Pies 32

bananas
Hogwarts House Meringues 92
Monster Book of Monsters 102

beets
"Happee Birthdae Harry" Cake 72
Hermione's Beaded Bag Cake 88
Nicolas Flamel's Parcels 34

big cakes
The Burrow Chocolate Cheesecake 112
Forbidden Forest Cake 74
"Happee Birthdae Harry" Cake 72
Hermione's Beaded Bag Cake 88
Hogwarts Gingerbread Castle 68
Honeydukes Haul Cake 78
Monster Book of Monsters 102

blueberries
Dark Detector Scones 48
Hogwarts House Meringues 92

Brazil nuts
Dragon-Roasted-Nut Tarts 60

breads
Deathly Hallows Bread 36
Devil's Snare Pretzel 38
Lightning Bolt Breads 12
Mandrake Bread 94
Mimbulus mimbletonia Bagel Loaf 16
Platform Nine and Three-Quarters Polenta Bake 52
Quidditch Pitch Focaccia 40
Salazar Slytherin's Sourdough Snake 18
Wand Breadsticks 14
Whomping Willow Cheese Straw 46

see also flatbreads; savory breads; sweet breads

bread crumbs
Halloumi Howlers 44
Hogwarts Treacle Tart 98

Brownie Cauldrons 80

brownies
Brownie Cauldrons 80

The Burrow Chocolate Cheesecake 112

C

carrots
House-Elf Carrot Cupcakes 86

cashews
Dragon-Roasted-Nut Tarts 60

celery
Great Hall Chicken Pie 56
Halloumi Howlers 44
Pumpkin Patch Pies 32

cheddar cheese
Hogwarts Crest Pie 24
Lightning Bolt Breads 12
Nimbus 2000 Crackers 26
Platform Nine and Three-Quarters Polenta Bake 52
Quidditch Pitch Focaccia 40

cheese
The Burrow Chocolate Cheesecake 112
Great Lake Tart 28
Halloumi Howlers 44
Hermione's Beaded Bag Cake 88
Hogwarts Crest Pie 24
Lightning Bolt Breads 12
Nimbus 2000 Crackers 26
Platform Nine and Three-Quarters Polenta Bake 52
Pumpkin Patch Pies 32
Quidditch Pitch Focaccia 40
Salazar Slytherin's Sourdough Snake 18
Sorting Hat Cupcakes 84
Time-Turner Crackers 50
Wand Breadsticks 14
Whomping Willow Cheese Straw 46

see also cheddar cheese; cream cheese; feta cheese; goat's cheese; Halloumi cheese; Parmesan cheese; Stilton; string cheese

cheesecake
  The Burrow Chocolate Cheesecake 112

cheese straw
  Whomping Willow Cheese Straw 46

chicken
  Great Hall Chicken Pie 56

chickpeas
  Nicolas Flamel's Parcels 34

chocolate
  Brownie Cauldrons 80
  The Burrow Chocolate Cheesecake 112
  Forbidden Forest Cake 74
  "Happee Birthdae Harry" Cake 72
  Hogwarts Gingerbread Castle 68
  House-Elf Carrot Cupcakes 86
  Mandrake Bread 94
  Sorting Hat Cupcakes 84
  Wizard's Chess Squares 90

choux pastry
  Puffskein Cream Puffs 108

cookies
  Fluttery Flying Key Cookies 100
  Gryffindor Sword Cookies 66
  Knitted Sweater Cookies 110
  Luna's Spectrespecs Cookies 64

crackers
  Nimbus 2000 Crackers 26
  Time-Turner Crackers 50

cream
  The Burrow Chocolate Cheesecake 112
  Forbidden Forest Cake 74
  Great Hall Chicken Pie 56
  Great Lake Tart 28
  Hogwarts House Meringues 92
  Puffskein Cream Puffs 108

cream cheese
  The Burrow Chocolate Cheesecake 112
  Hermione's Beaded Bag Cake 88
  Quidditch Pitch Focaccia 40
  Salazar Slytherin's Sourdough Snake 18
  Sorting Hat Cupcakes 84

cucumber
  Salazar Slytherin's Sourdough Snake 18

cupcakes
  House-Elf Carrot Cupcakes 86
  Sorting Hat Cupcakes 84

custard
  Puffskein Cream Puffs 108

D
Dark Detector Scones 48

Deathly Hallows Bread 36

desserts
  The Burrow Chocolate Cheesecake 112
  Hogwarts Treacle Tart 98

Devil's Snare Pretzel 38

Dragon-Roasted-Nut Tarts 60

Dumbledore's Sherbet Lemon Rolls 106

E
eggs
  The Burrow Chocolate Cheesecake 112
  Dark Detector Scones 48
  Dragon-Roasted-Nut Tarts 60
  Dumbledore's Sherbet Lemon Rolls 106
  Fluttery Flying Key Cookies 100
  Forbidden Forest Cake 74
  Great Hall Chicken Pie 56
  Great Lake Tart 28
  Gryffindor Sword Cookies 66
  Hagrid's Hut Rock Cakes 82
  Halloumi Howlers 44
  Hermione's Beaded Bag Cake 88
  Hogwarts Crest Pie 24
  Hogwarts Gingerbread Castle 68
  Hogwarts House Meringues 92
  Hogwarts Treacle Tart 98
  House-Elf Carrot Cupcakes 86
  Knitted Sweater Cookies 110
  Luna's Spectrespecs Cookies 64
  Mandrake Bread 94
  Mimbulus mimbletonia Bagel Loaf 16
  Monster Book of Monsters 102
  Nicolas Flamel's Parcels 34
  Nimbus 2000 Crackers 26
  Platform Nine and Three-Quarters Polenta Bake 52
  Puffskein Cream Puffs 108
  Pumpkin Patch Pies 32
  Salazar Slytherin's Sourdough Snake 18
  Sorting Hat Cupcakes 84
  Time-Turner Crackers 50
  Whomping Willow Cheese Straw 46
  Wizarding Hats 22
  Yorkshire Delights 58

  see also egg whites; egg yolks

eggplant
  Halloumi Howlers 44
  Hogwarts Crest Pie 24

egg whites
  Dragon-Roasted-Nut Tarts 60
  Fluttery Flying Key Cookies 100
  Gryffindor Sword Cookies 66
  Hogwarts House Meringues 92
  Luna's Spectrespecs Cookies 64

egg yolks
  Great Lake Tart 28

Halloumi Howlers 44
Hermione's Beaded Bag
Cake 88
Hogwarts Crest Pie 24
Hogwarts Gingerbread
Castle 68
Hogwarts Treacle Tart 98
Knitted Sweater Cookies 110
Luna's Spectrespecs Cookies 64
Nimbus 2000 Crackers 26
Puffskein Cream Puffs 108
Pumpkin Patch Pies 32
Sorting Hat Cupcakes 84
Time-Turner Crackers 50

F

feta cheese
Pumpkin Patch Pies 32

filo pastry
Halloumi Howlers 44

flatbreads
Lightning Bolt Breads 12
Quidditch Pitch Focaccia 40

Fluttery Flying Key Cookies 100

Forbidden Forest Cake 74

fruit
Dark Detector Scones 48
Hogwarts House Meringues 92
Savory Owl Muffins 30
Time-Turner Crackers 50
Wizard's Chess Squares 90

see also bananas; blueberries; grapes; kiwi fruit; oranges; raspberries

G

garlic
Devil's Snare Pretzel 38
Great Lake Tart 28
Halloumi Howlers 44
Nicolas Flamel's Parcels 34
Quidditch Pitch Focaccia 40

ginger
Hogwarts Gingerbread
Castle 68
Knitted Sweater Cookies 110

gingerbread
Hogwarts Gingerbread
Castle 68

gluten-free
Dragon-Roasted-Nut Tarts 60
Fluttery Flying Key Cookies 100
Forbidden Forest Cake 74
Hogwarts House Meringues 92
House-Elf Carrot Cupcakes 86
Knitted Sweater Cookies 110
Nicolas Flamel's Parcels 34
Platform Nine and Three-
Quarters Polenta Bake 52
Savory Owl Muffins 30
Wizard's Chess Squares 90

goat cheese
Time-Turner Crackers 50

grapes
Savory Owl Muffins 30
Time-Turner Crackers 50

Great Hall Chicken Pie 56

Great Lake Tart 28

Greek yogurt
Deathly Hallows Bread 36
Dragon-Roasted-Nut Tarts 60

Gryffindor Sword Cookies 66

H

Hagrid's Hut Rock Cakes 82

Halloumi cheese
Halloumi Howlers 44

Halloumi Howlers 44

**"Happee Birthdae Harry"
Cake 72**

hazelnuts
Dragon-Roasted-Nut Tarts 60
Fluttery Flying Key
Cookies 100

Hermione's Beaded Bag Cake 88

Hogwarts Crest Pie 24

Hogwarts Gingerbread Castle 68

Hogwarts House Meringues 92

Hogwarts Treacle Tart 98

honey
Nicolas Flamel's Parcels 34
Time-Turner Crackers 50
Wizard's Chess Squares 90

honeycomb
Puffskein Cream Puffs 108

Honeydukes Haul Cake 78

House-Elf Carrot Cupcakes 86

I

individual bakes
Brownie Cauldrons 80
Dark Detector Scones 48
Dragon-Roasted-Nut Tarts 60
Dumbledore's Sherbet Lemon
Rolls 106
Fluttery Flying Key Cookies 100
Gryffindor Sword Cookies 66
Hagrid's Hut Rock Cakes 82
Halloumi Howlers 44
Hogwarts House Meringues 92
House-Elf Carrot Cupcakes 86
Knitted Sweater Cookies 110
Lightning Bolt Breads 12
Luna's Spectrespecs Cookies 64
Nicolas Flamel's Parcels 34
Nimbus 2000 Crackers 26
Puffskein Cream Puffs 108
Pumpkin Patch Pies 32
Savory Owl Muffins 30
Sorting Hat Cupcakes 84

Time-Turner Crackers   50
Wand Breadsticks   14
Wizarding Hats   22
Wizard's Chess Squares   90
Yorkshire Delights   58

J
jam
Honeydukes Haul Cake   78

K
kitchen safety   8

kiwi fruit
Hogwarts House Meringues   92

Knitted Sweater Cookies   110

L
lemons
Hagrid's Hut Rock Cakes   82
Hogwarts Treacle Tart   98

Lightning Bolt Breads   12

Luna's Spectrespecs Cookies   64

M
Mandrake Bread   94

maple syrup
Wizard's Chess Squares   90

meat
Great Hall Chicken Pie   56
Great Lake Tart   28
Pumpkin Patch Pies   32
Wizarding Hats   22
Yorkshire Delights   58

see also bacon; chicken; mince beef; sausages

meringues
Hogwarts House Meringues   92

milk
Dark Detector Scones   48

Deathly Hallows Bread   36
Dumbledore's Sherbet Lemon Rolls   106
Forbidden Forest Cake   74
Great Lake Tart   28
Hagrid's Hut Rock Cakes   82
Honeydukes Haul Cake   78
Mandrake Bread   94
Puffskein Cream Puffs   108
Yorkshire Delights   58

Mimbulus mimbletonia **Bagel Loaf**   16

minced beef
Yorkshire Delights   58

Monster Book of Monsters   102

muffins, savory
Savory Owl Muffins   30

mushrooms
Great Hall Chicken Pie   56

N
Nicolas Flamel's Parcels   34

Nimbus 2000 Crackers   26

nuts
Brownie Cauldrons   80
Dragon-Roasted-Nut Tarts   60
Fluttery Flying Key Cookies   100
Mandrake Bread   94
Salazar Slytherin's Sourdough Snake   18

see also almonds; Brazil nuts; cashews; hazelnuts; pecans; walnuts

O
oat milk
Savory Owl Muffins   30
Wand Breadsticks   14

oats
Wizard's Chess Squares   90

olives
Quidditch Pitch Focaccia   40

onions
Deathly Hallows Bread   36
Great Hall Chicken Pie   56
Great Lake Tart   28
Halloumi Howlers   44
Hogwarts Crest Pie   24
Nicolas Flamel's Parcels   34
Nimbus 2000 Crackers   26
Platform Nine and Three-Quarters Polenta Bake   52
Pumpkin Patch Pies   32

see also red onions; scallions

oranges
Wizard's Chess Squares   90

P
Parmesan cheese
Time-Turner Crackers   50
Whomping Willow Cheese Straw   46

pastry
Dragon-Roasted-Nut Tarts   60
Great Hall Chicken Pie   56
Great Lake Tart   28
Halloumi Howlers   44
Hogwarts Crest Pie   24
Hogwarts Treacle Tart   98
Nicolas Flamel's Parcels   34
Puffskein Cream Puffs   108
Pumpkin Patch Pies   32
Whomping Willow Cheese Straw   46
Wizarding Hats   22

see also filo pastry; pies; puff pastry; shortcrust pastry

pea shoots
Pumpkin Patch Pies   32

pecans
Brownie Cauldrons   80
Dragon-Roasted-Nut Tarts   60

peppers
  Deathly Hallows Bread   36
  Hogwarts Crest Pie   24
  Mimbulus mimbletonia Bagel Loaf   16
  Savory Owl Muffins   30

pies
  Great Hall Chicken Pie   56
  Hogwarts Crest Pie   24
  Pumpkin Patch Pies   32

Platform Nine and Three-Quarters Polenta Bake   52

polenta
  Platform Nine and Three-Quarters Polenta Bake   52

potatoes
  Dark Detector Scones   48

puff pastry
  Dragon-Roasted-Nut Tarts   60
  Hogwarts Crest Pie   24
  Whomping Willow Cheese Straw   46
  Wizarding Hats   22

Puffskein Cream Puffs   108

Pumpkin Patch Pies   32

Q
Quidditch Pitch Focaccia   40

R
radishes
  Savory Owl Muffins   30

raisins
  House-Elf Carrot Cupcakes   86

raspberries
  Hogwarts House Meringues   92

red onions
  Halloumi Howlers   44

rolls
  Dumbledore's Sherbet Lemon Rolls   106

S
Salazar Slytherin's Sourdough Snake   18

sausages, breakfast
  Wizarding Hats   22

savory breads
  Deathly Hallows Bread   36
  Devil's Snare Pretzel   38
  Mimbulus mimbletonia Bagel Loaf   16
  Salazar Slytherin's Sourdough Snake   18
  Wand Breadsticks   14

Savory Owl Muffins   30

scallions
  Nimbus 2000 Crackers   26
  Platform Nine and Three-Quarters Polenta Bake   52

scones, savory
  Dark Detector Scones   48

shallots
  Yorkshire Delights   58

shortcrust pastry
  Great Hall Chicken Pie   56
  Great Lake Tart   28
  Hogwarts Treacle Tart   98
  Nicolas Flamel's Parcels   34
  Pumpkin Patch Pies   32

small cakes
  Brownie Cauldrons   80
  Dumbledore's Sherbet Lemon Rolls   106
  Hagrid's Hut Rock Cakes   82
  House-Elf Carrot Cupcakes   86
  Puffskein Cream Puffs   108
  Sorting Hat Cupcakes   84

snacks
  Dark Detector Scones   48
  Devil's Snare Pretzel   38
  Dragon-Roasted-Nut Tarts   60
  Fluttery Flying Key Cookies   100
  Gryffindor Sword Cookies   66
  Hagrid's Hut Rock Cakes   82
  Knitted Sweater Cookies   110
  Lightning Bolt Breads   12
  Luna's Spectrespecs Cookies   64
  Nimbus 2000 Crackers   26
  Savory Owl Muffins   30
  Time-Turner Crackers   50
  Wand Breadsticks   14
  Wizarding Hats   22
  Wizard's Chess Squares   90

Sorting Hat Cupcakes   84

spinach
  Halloumi Howlers   44

Stilton
  Great Lake Tart   28

string cheese
  Nimbus 2000 Crackers   26

sultanas
  House-Elf Carrot Cupcakes   86

sweet breads
  Mandrake Bread   94

sweet corn
  Great Lake Tart   28
  Platform Nine and Three-Quarters Polenta Bake   52

sweet potatoes
  Devil's Snare Pretzel   38
  Savory Owl Muffins   30

T
tarts
  Dragon-Roasted-Nut Tarts   60
  Great Lake Tart   28
  Hogwarts Treacle Tart   98

Time-Turner Crackers   50

tomatoes
   Quidditch Pitch Focaccia   40

V

vanilla extract
   Forbidden Forest Cake   74
   "Happee Birthdae Harry" Cake   72
   Honeydukes Haul Cake   78
   Luna's Spectrespecs Cookies   64
   Mandrake Bread   94
   Monster Book of Monsters   102
   Puffskein Cream Puffs   108

vegan
   Brownie Cauldrons   80
   Devil's Snare Pretzel   38
   "Happee Birthdae Harry" Cake   72
   Lightning Bolt Breads   12
   Quidditch Pitch Focaccia   40
   Salazar Slytherin's Sourdough Snake   18
   Savory Owl Muffins   30
   Wand Breadsticks   14
   Wizard's Chess Squares   90

vegetarian
   Brownie Cauldrons   80
   The Burrow Chocolate Cheesecake   112
   Dark Detector Scones   48
   Deathly Hallows Bread   36
   Devil's Snare Pretzel   38
   Dragon-Roasted-Nut Tarts   60
   Dumbledore's Sherbet Lemon Rolls   106
   Fluttery Flying Key Cookies   100
   Great Lake Tart   28
   Gryffindor Sword Cookies   66
   Hagrid's Hut Rock Cakes   82
   Halloumi Howlers   44
   "Happee Birthdae Harry" Cake   72
   Hermione's Beaded Bag Cake   88
   Hogwarts Crest Pie   24
   Hogwarts Gingerbread Castle   68

Hogwarts House Meringues   92
Hogwarts Treacle Tart   98
House-Elf Carrot Cupcakes   86
Knitted Sweater Cookies   110
Lightning Bolt Breads   12
Luna's Spectrespecs Cookies   64
Mandrake Bread   94
Mimbulus mimbletonia Bagel Loaf   16
Monster Book of Monsters   102
Nicolas Flamel's Parcels   34
Nimbus 2000 Crackers   26
Platform Nine and Three-Quarters Polenta Bake   52
Puffskein Cream Puffs   108
Pumpkin Patch Pies   32
Quidditch Pitch Focaccia   40
Salazar Slytherin's Sourdough Snake   18
Savory Owl Muffins   30
Sorting Hat Cupcakes   84
Time-Turner Crackers   50
Wand Breadsticks   14
Whomping Willow Cheese Straw   46
Wizarding Hats   22
Wizard's Chess Squares   90
Yorkshire Delights   58

W

walnuts
   Brownie Cauldrons   80
   Dragon-Roasted-Nut Tarts   60

Wand Breadsticks   14

watercress
   Pumpkin Patch Pies   32

Whomping Willow Cheese Straw   46

Wizarding Hats   22
Wizard's Chess Squares   90

Y

Yorkshire Delights   58

Z

zucchini
   Great Lake Tart   28
   Hogwarts Crest Pie   24
   Savory Owl Muffins   30

Copyright © 2021 Warner Bros. Entertainment Inc.
WIZARDING WORLD characters, names and related indicia are © & ™ Warner Bros. Entertainment Inc. WB SHIELD: © & ™ WBEI. Publishing Rights © JKR. (s21)

All rights reserved. Published by Scholastic Inc. *Publishers since 1920.* SCHOLASTIC and associated logos are trademarks and/or registered trademarks of Scholastic Inc.

The publisher does not have any control over and does not assume any responsibility for author, or third-party websites, or their content.

No part of this publication may be reproduced, stored in a retrieval system, or transmitted in any form, or by any means, electronic, mechanical, photocopying, recording, or otherwise, without written permission of the publisher. For information regarding permission, write to Scholastic Inc., Attention: Permissions Department, 557 Broadway, New York, NY 10012.

ISBN 978-1-338-28526-0

14 13 12 11 10 9   24 25 26 27

Printed in China 62

First printing 2021

Supplementary imagery © Shutterstock

AMAZING15, Project Management and Design
JOANNA FARROW, Writer and Food Styling
KATE LLOYD, Additional Writing and Copy Editing
LIZ & MAX HAARALA HAMILTON, Photography
DOMINIQUE ELOÏSE ALEXANDER, Prop Styling (and Harry Potter super fan!)
MAUD EDEN, Food Styling

Thank you to our models:
Coco, Ejim, Faith, Lorraine, and Mikey

Special thanks to:
Kevin Pettman, Dan Scudamore, and Alysia Scudamore at Urban Angels

ERINN PASCAL, Editor, Scholastic
JESSICA MELTZER, Senior Designer, Scholastic
SUSAN LEE, Senior Production Editor, Scholastic
VICTORIA SELOVER, Director – Editorial Publishing, Warner Bros.
KATIE CAMPBELL, Senior Design Manager – Global Publishing, Warner Bros.
RACHEL MOORHEAD, Product Development Executive – The Blair Partnership